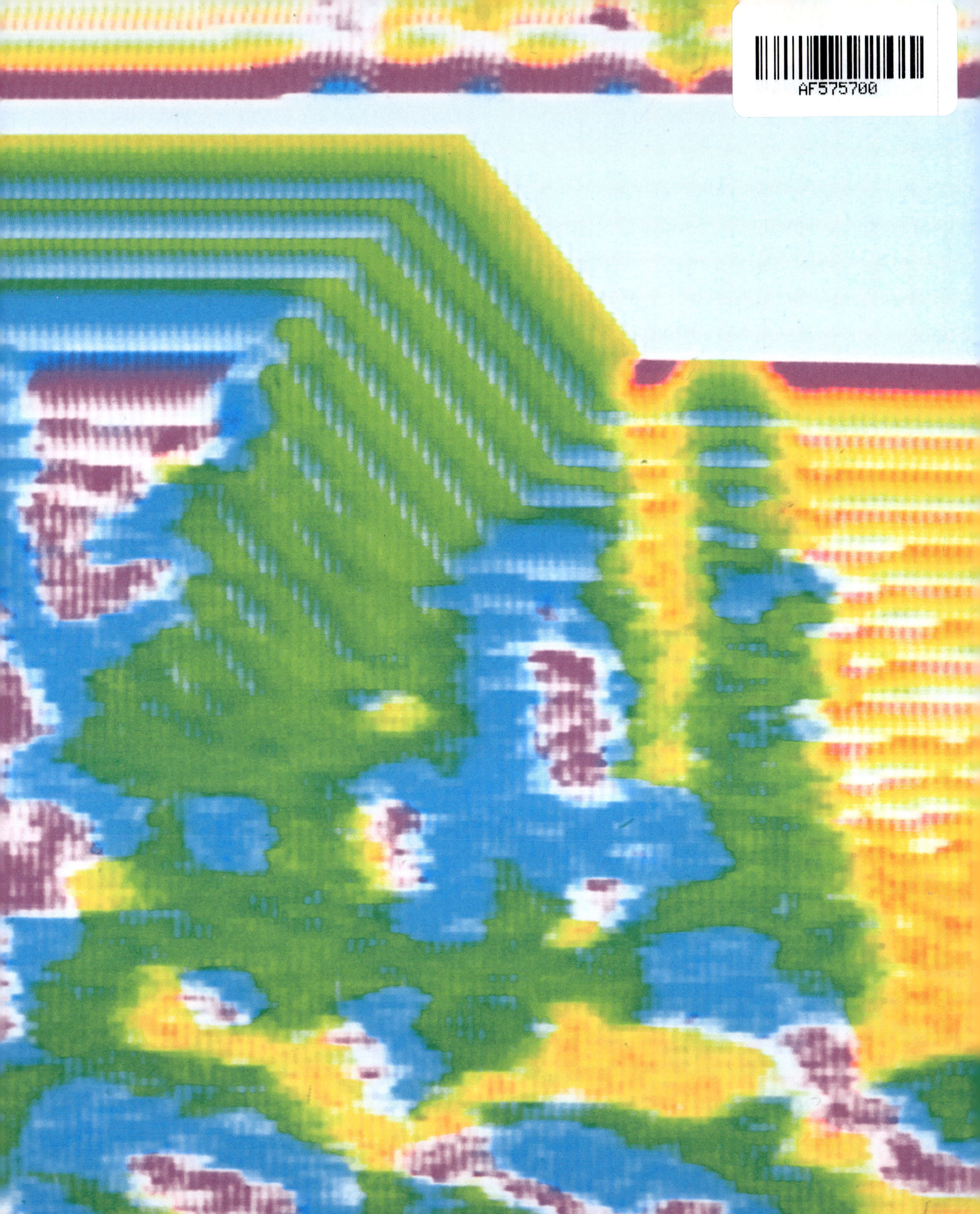

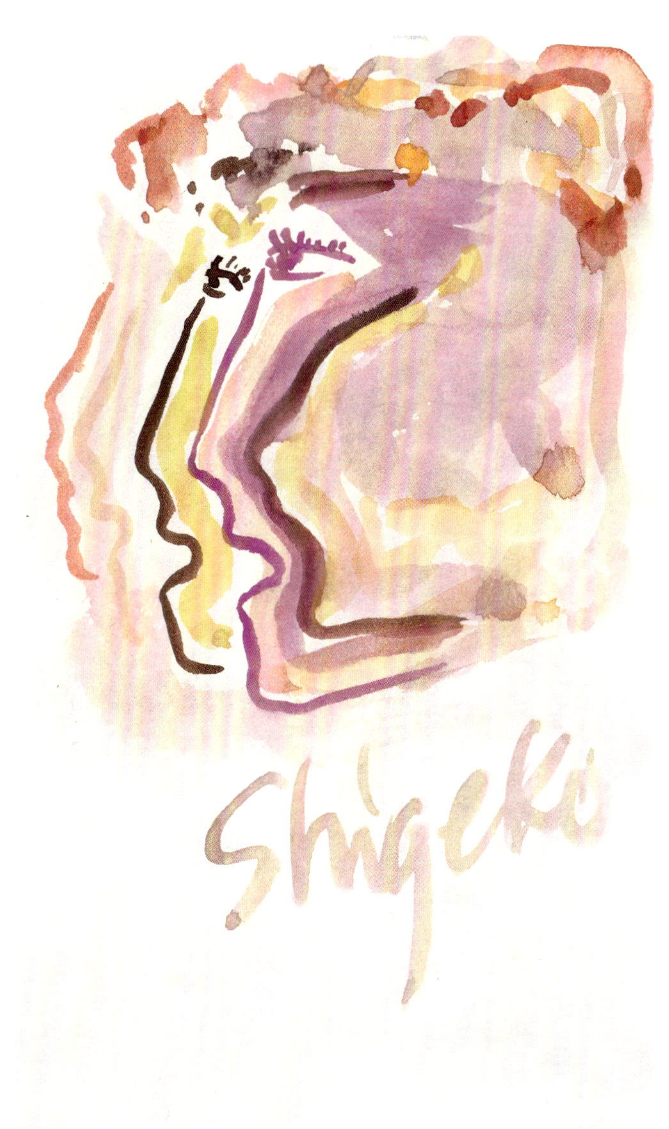
Shigeko

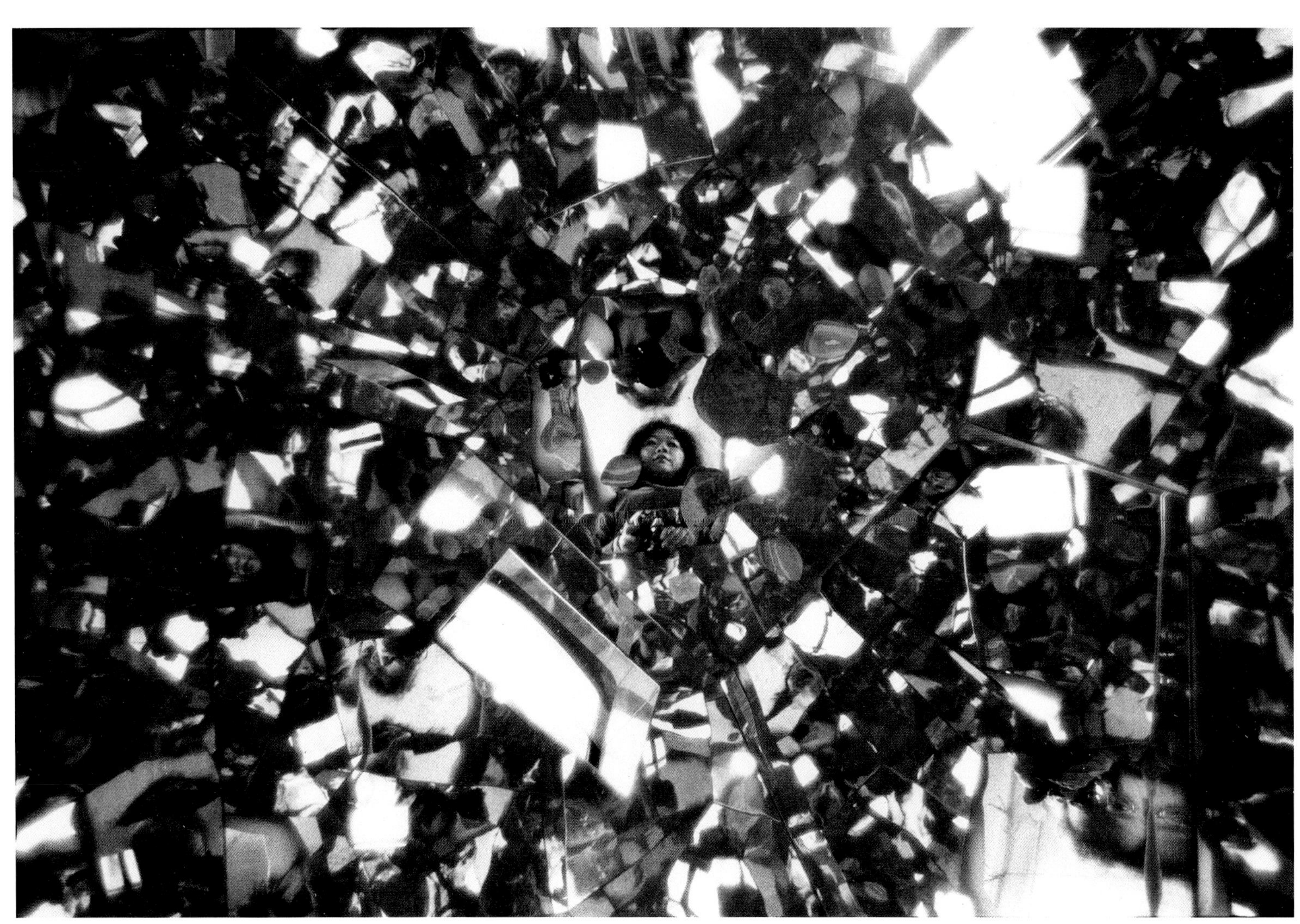

Shigeko Kubota Liquid Reality

Erica Papernik-Shimizu

With an essay by Gloria Sutton

The Museum of Modern Art, New York

Hyundai Card

Hyundai Card is delighted to support this presentation of the work of revolutionary artist Shigeko Kubota, whose pioneering video sculptures transformed how artists approach media-based art. Kubota's use of video technology to document her life and transcultural identity and her remarkable ability to bridge cultural divides established her as a distinguished member of the first generation of video artists. Her feminist perspective, strengthened by her unique poetic sensibility, helped her formulate a visual style that is unlike that of any other artist of her time. Hyundai Card is committed to supporting the work of visionaries like Kubota, whose legacy continues to stimulate dialogue about interdisciplinary art and technology.

Hyundai Card believes art has the power to enrich people's lives. In this regard, we are proud to partner with The Museum of Modern Art, supporting its mission to connect people with art. A leading premium credit card issuer in Seoul, Korea, Hyundai Card has been keeping up with crucial movements in culture, society, and technologies to deliver meaningful experiences to customers and inspire them. Four Hyundai Card libraries in Seoul dedicated to different themes—design, travel, music, and cooking—are part of these efforts. We pledge to remain committed to providing innovative digital products and services as well as unique card plate design and cultural activities.

Contents

Foreword

This publication accompanies the first exhibition of the work of Shigeko Kubota at a museum in the United States in twenty-five years. Kubota was one of the first artists to commit to video and pioneered the multidisciplinary medium of video sculpture. This show focuses on a selection of pivotal video sculptures, made between the early 1970s and the mid-1980s, that are particularly resonant today in their exploration of identity, technology, and the natural world. It is fitting that this presentation take place at The Museum of Modern Art, as Kubota was involved in several significant moments in the Museum's history, starting in 1970, when one of her photographs of the infamous chess match between John Cage and Marcel Duchamp was included in Kynaston McShine's groundbreaking *Information* show. Her *Video Poem* (1970–75) was included in *Rooms*, the inaugural exhibition at MoMA PS1 (then the Institute of Art and Urban Resources), organized by Alanna Heiss in 1976. And her *Duchampiana: Nude Descending a Staircase* (1976) was featured in a 1978 exhibition organized by Barbara London as part of the Projects series, then a relatively new program dedicated to presenting works by emerging artists. The acquisition of *Nude* in 1981—the first video sculpture to enter MoMA's collection—signaled a new era in the Museum's approach to moving-image-based artworks. In the decades that followed, the Museum amassed a substantial collection of Kubota's single-channel Broken Diary videos, and, in 2008, as part of the watershed Gilbert and Lila Silverman Fluxus Collection Gift, MoMA acquired works and ephemera from the artist's influential Fluxus period. Today, we are proud to celebrate the recent acquisition of Kubota's *Berlin Diary: Thanks to My Ancestors* (1981), which was generously supported by The Modern Women's Fund.

This brief history exemplifies the Museum's commitment to representing key artists' work in depth, a strategy that is at the core of MoMA's redoubled efforts to enrich and expand the stories the collection can tell. The present exhibition also extends the Museum's longstanding research into the Japanese avant-garde, which yielded the 2012 exhibition *Tokyo 1955–1970: A New Avant-Garde* and continues in the work of the Contemporary and Modern Art Perspectives (C-MAP) Asia Group. This presentation additionally intersects with MoMA's sustained dedication to foregrounding the essential role that women have played in the history of video art, as seen in the recent acquisitions of early works by Steina Vasulka, Beryl Korot, Dara Birnbaum, and Gretchen Bender, among others.

We applaud Erica Papernik-Shimizu, Associate Curator, Department of Media and Performance, for skillfully and thoughtfully organizing this exhibition. From the initial conversations about this project, the Shigeko Kubota Video Art Foundation has been a true collaborator, generously opening up its archives to us and sharing its insights and expertise. I also extend my gratitude to Gloria Sutton for her illuminating contribution to this catalogue.

Finally, on behalf of the staff and the trustees of the Museum, I would like to sincerely thank Hyundai Card for providing essential support for this exhibition. The Jill and Peter Kraus Endowed Fund for Contemporary Exhibitions provided major support. The Lonti Ebers Endowment for Performance and the Sarah Arison Endowment Fund for Performance also provided generous funding.

Glenn D. Lowry
The David Rockefeller Director
The Museum of Modern Art

Acknowledgments

The development of this exhibition and catalogue has benefited from the support of many incredible people, both in and outside The Museum of Modern Art. First and foremost, I am indebted to the Shigeko Kubota Video Art Foundation for its generous loans to the exhibition. I am especially grateful to Norman L. Ballard, Director, for his complete devotion to "the cause" and his steadfast encouragement from the start. Lia Robinson, Director of Research and Programs, openly imparted her wealth of knowledge during many late-night and early-morning conversations, and Reid N. Ballard, Director of Collections and Exhibitions, who has played a key role in preserving Kubota's work, made it readily accessible to me during a global pandemic. Jochen Saueracker, Art Director and Archivist, provided essential insight. Additional thanks to Kevin Harrison, Director of Infrastructure and Facilities. I wish to acknowledge the Foundation's distinguished Advisors: Paul Garrin, Robert Harris, Wulf Herzogenrath, Barbara Hoffman, Esq., Solha Kim, Jung Sung Lee, Barbara London, Mary Lucier, Barbara Moore, Mark Patsfall, Juan Puente, David A. Ross, Carl Solway, Toni Stooss, Reiko Tomii, Midori Yoshimoto, and Lori Zippay. I recognize the Foundation's exceptional team of artisans: Christian Draheim, Jesse Farrenkoph, Paul Garrin, Daniel Hartnet, Dean Kozelek, Chi Tien Lui, Jon Reichert, Maurice Schechter, and Kazumi Tanaka.

At MoMA, I thank Glenn D. Lowry, The David Rockefeller Director, for his commitment to visionary artists and his unwavering support of the Media and Performance program. Ramona Bannayan, former Senior Deputy Director of Exhibitions and Collections, ensured the exhibition's success. Sarah Suzuki, Deputy Director of Curatorial Affairs, enthusiastically championed this endeavor, which also benefited from the leadership of Todd Bishop, former Senior Deputy Director of External Affairs, and James Gara, Chief Operating Officer. As ever, I am grateful for the tremendous commitment of the Committee on Media and Performance. I extend my deepest gratitude to Stuart Comer, The Lonti Ebers Chief Curator of Media and Performance, who advocated for the importance of this project in ways big and small, and offered treasured guidance.

This project was built on the inspiring work of numerous individuals and institutions. I offer my warmest thanks to Gloria Sutton, Associate Professor of Contemporary Art History, Northeastern University, for her essay, which skillfully interlaces the many strands of Kubota's practice in a fresh take on the artist's legacy. I am grateful to Barbara London, mentor and friend, who brought video art to MoMA and advocated for Kubota's work early on. It is crucial to acknowledge Electronic Arts Intermix, New York, whose stewardship of Kubota's single-channel videos has spanned more than five decades. I thank Lori Zippay, former Executive Director, for championing Kubota's work and for sharing her research. Rebecca Cleman, Executive Director, enthusiastically supported this project, as did her colleagues Karl McCool and Jon Dieringer. I am also grateful to Midori Yoshimoto, Associate Professor of Art History and Gallery Director, New Jersey City University, for her scholarship. Thanks also to Mayumi Hamada, Curator, Niigata Prefectural Museum of Modern Art, for her support.

Protagonists in the field who generously shared their firsthand experiences and provided research support include Debora Bernagozzi, Signal Culture; Peer Bode; Sherry Miller Hocking, Experimental Television Center; Chris King, Tate; John Klacsmann, Anthology Film Archives; Mary Lucier; and Takako Okamoto, Estate of Takehisa Kosugi. I am grateful to

Jon Hendricks for his kindness over many years. Special thanks go to Hubert Winter and Natascha Burger, Galerie Hubert Winter. I also thank the institutions that shared images and archival material: Aspen Art Museum, Berkeley Art Museum/Pacific Film Archives, Binghamton University, CalArts, Everson Museum of Art, Fondazione Mudima, The Kitchen, Long Beach Museum of Art, Milwaukee Museum of Art, MIT List Visual Arts Center, San Francisco Art Institute, SculptureCenter, Stedelijk Museum Amsterdam, Walker Art Center, White Columns, and the Whitney Museum of American Art.

I acknowledge the individuals whose photographs are reproduced in this publication, including Peer Bode, Peter Butler, Evangelos Dousmanis, Peter Harris, Eric Kroll, Hollis Melton, Peter Moore, Hiroshi Naruse, Bobby Rogers, Stephan Reusse, Simon Veres, and John Wronn. My sincere gratitude goes to Barbara Moore, whose generous support at the height of the pandemic was indispensable to this publication. Kris Graves, Achim Kukulies, and Daniel Salemi captured new images for this book. Satomi Matsuzaki, Lara Mones, Lia Robinson, Michi Shimizu, Masahiro Takahashi, and Etsuko Thow kindly assisted with translating Japanese texts into English. Special thanks to Kaoru Mochizuki, *Bijutsu techo*.

This catalogue was produced in collaboration with MoMA's Department of Publications. Don McMahon, Editorial Director, and Curtis R. Scott, Associate Publisher, provided crucial guidance. Marc Sapir, Production Director, made the images sparkle, and I have learned much from him in the process of building this book. Amanda Washburn, Senior Designer, created an inspired design that allows the works to speak for themselves, and I am thankful for her kindness. Maria Marchenkova, Senior Assistant Editor, brought her talent, grace, and reassuring sense of humor to the editing of this volume. Rebecca Roberts, Editor, also lent her sharp eye at the last stage. Thanks are due to Naomi Falk, Rights Coordinator; Hannah Kim, Business and Marketing Director; and Sophie Golub, Department Manager, for their careful oversight. Mary Jane Jacob, Professor and Director, Institute for Curatorial Research and Practice, School of the Art Institute of Chicago, served as an early reader, and her comments improved the book.

I have benefited greatly from interdepartmental collaboration at MoMA. Christophe Cherix, The Robert Lehman Foundation Chief Curator of Drawings and Prints, and Ann Temkin, The Marie-Josée and Henry Kravis Chief Curator of Painting and Sculpture, granted key loans. In the Department of Drawings and Prints, I thank Danielle Johnson, Curatorial Assistant; Emily Cushman, Collection Specialist; and Kunbi Oni, Collection Specialist, Acquisitions. In the Department of Painting and Sculpture, Cara Manes, Associate Curator, and Lily Goldberg, Collection Specialist, offered collegial advice.

I am immensely appreciative of the remarkable work of my colleagues across the Museum. For securing support, I am grateful to Maggie Lyko, Director, and Sylvia Renner, Associate Director, Special Events and Affiliate Programs; Jessica Smith, Assistant Director of Institutional Giving, Global Partnerships; and Olivia Mitchell, Associate Director of Development. For their invaluable expertise and impactful research in readying the artworks for exhibition, I am indebted to my colleagues in the David Booth Conservation Department, led by Kate Lewis, The Agnes Gund Chief Conservator: Peter Oleksik, Associate Media Conservator; Amy Brost, Assistant Media Conservator; Lia Kramer, Andrew W. Mellon Fellow in Media Conservation; Megan Randall, Associate Objects Conservator; and Andy Wolf, David Booth Fellow in Objects Conservation. I thank Rob Jung, Manager, and Tom Krueger, Assistant Manager, Art Handling and Preparation, for their meticulous work and enthusiasm. Special thanks to Peter Perez, Frame Shop Foreman. I am grateful to my colleagues in Exhibition Design and Production:

Lana Hum, Director; Hiroko Ishikawa, Exhibition Designer, who brought her inspired vision and razor-sharp precision to the exhibition's design; Matthew Cox, Senior Production Manager; and Mack Cole-Edelsack, Senior Design Manager. In the Audio Visual department, I want to thank Aaron Louis, Director; Aaron Harrow, Audio Visual Design Manager; Paul DiPietro, Technical Manager; and Mike Gibbons, Audio Visual Exhibitions Foreperson, all of whom helped to realize this project and shared their expert technical knowledge. Travis Kray, AV Tech, provided essential support.

In the Department of Exhibition Planning and Administration, led by Erik Patton, Director, my heartfelt thanks go to Maya Taylor, Exhibition and Budget Assistant, whose guidance and enthusiasm were instrumental to this project from start to finish. I am also grateful to Jennifer Cohen, Associate Director, for her counsel. In the Department of Collection Management and Exhibition Registration, led by Stefanii Ruta Atkins, Head Registrar, I want to acknowledge Sacha Eaton, Associate Registrar, who worked on this exhibition, and Sarah Primm, Assistant Registrar, who cares for the Department of Media and Performance collection, as well as Sydney Briggs, Associate Registrar, and Kathleen Hill, Registrar. I am grateful to the Department of Archives, Library, and Research Collections, led by Michelle Elligott, and especially Elisabeth Thomas, Assistant Archivist. Thanks are also due to Amanda Hicks, Director of Communications and Public Affairs, and Maureen Masters, Publicist. On the Creative Team, I thank Leah Dickerman, former Director of Editorial Content and Strategy; Rob Baker, Director of Marketing and Creative Strategy; Rebecca Stokes, Director of Marketing Campaigns and Audience Engagement; Jason Persse, Editorial Manager; Alex Halberstadt, Senior Writer; Claire Corey, Production Manager; Damien Saatdjian, Art Director; and David Klein, Senior Designer. In the Department of Education, I am grateful to Sara Bodinson, Director of Interpretation, Research, and Digital Learning, and Francesca Rosenberg, Director of Community, Access, and School Programs. I also wish to thank Ava Childers, Assistant General Counsel, for her sound advice; Sarah Stewart, Office of the Senior Deputy Director of Exhibitions and Collections; Jennifer Sellar, Digital Assets Manager; Robert Kastler, Director of Imaging and Visual Resources; Sonya Shrier, Director of Visitor Engagement; Tunji Adeniji, Chief Facilities and Safety Officer; Daniel Platt, Director of Security; and Tyrone Wyllie, Associate Director of Security.

The talents, meticulous research, and thoughtful contributions of Veronika Molnar, who went above and beyond during her seven-month internship, are reflected throughout this book. I am ever grateful to my colleague and friend Danielle A. Jackson, former Curatorial Assistant, who generously consulted on this publication with impeccable insight and imagination. I warmly acknowledge the entire Department of Media and Performance: Ana Janevski, Thomas J. Lax, Rebecca Kusovitsky, Martha Joseph, Chelsea Airey, Lilia Taboada, and Piper Marshall. I would like to extend a special thanks to my former colleagues Giampaolo Bianconi, Athena Christa Holbrook, and Stephanie Weber.

My final thanks are reserved for the Papernik, Shimizu, and Stein families (Madelyn for her keen eye), and for Trevor, Goldie, and Akiva for their boundless wisdom and care.

Erica Papernik-Shimizu
Associate Curator, Department of
Media and Performance

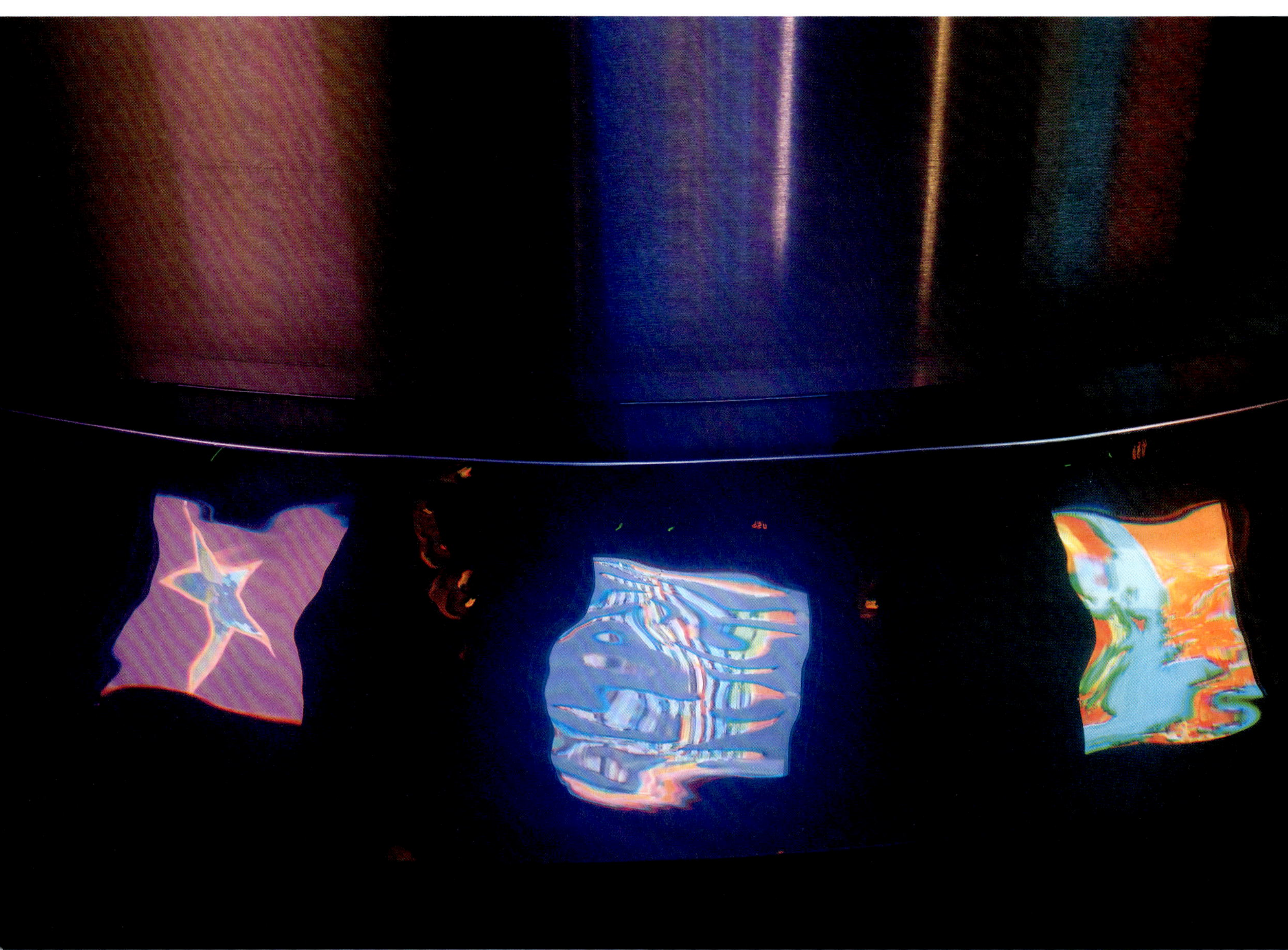

Fig. 1. *River* (detail). 1979–81. Three-channel standard-definition video (color, silent; approx. 32 min. each), three cathode-ray tube monitors, stainless steel, plastic mirrors, water, and wave machine, overall dimensions variable, basin: 22 × 9 × 4 ft. (670.6 × 274.3 × 121.9 cm). Shigeko Kubota Video Art Foundation. Installed in *Before Projection: Video Sculpture 1974–1995*, MIT List Visual Arts Center, Cambridge, Massachusetts, February 8–April 15, 2018

Erica Papernik-Shimizu

Introduction

Describing the moving images in her work *River* (1979–81) (fig. 1; see also pages 68–77), which consist of colorized footage of herself swimming and electronically generated graphics, Shigeko Kubota mused, "Once cast into video's reality, infinite variation becomes possible . . . freedom to dissolve, reconstruct, mutate all forms, shape, color, location, speed, scale . . . liquid reality."[1] Kubota first alluded to this notion of absolute freedom, which would prove central to her lifelong dedication to the expansion of art, in a small untitled painting she made in 1965 (fig. 2) that still hangs in the loft in New York's SoHo district where she lived with her husband, the artist Nam June Paik, and which now houses the Shigeko Kubota Video Art Foundation.[2] On the canvas is a Zen Buddhist phrase, rendered in loosely drawn Japanese characters, that translates literally as "moving clouds, flowing water" and conveys a state of openness to all possibilities.[3] In Zen, to be enlightened is to be "without a dwelling place" in the broadest sense, untethered from any place, but also from societal expectations and the systems of perception we typically regard as "real"—concepts with which Kubota, who described herself as "of a religious Buddhist family," with connections to monastic life on her father's side, would have been familiar.[4] She made this painting soon after emigrating from Tokyo, where she had been active in the avant-garde scene, to New York City, drawn to its "glittering" art world and the robust activity of Fluxus in particular.[5] Kubota had encountered many of the movement's protagonists while in Japan; its utopian vision, which privileged the everyday over the virtuosic, and its embrace of the indeterminacy pioneered by John Cage—with whom she would later collaborate[6]—were formative influences. She had struck up a correspondence with George Maciunas, Fluxus's founder, who encouraged her to move to New York and even met her at the airport upon her arrival (fig. 3).[7] Stateside, Kubota quickly became a key member of the Fluxus community, and her legacy has largely been shaped by this association, particularly through the mythologizing of her contribution to the Perpetual Fluxfest in 1965: her first and last solo performance, *Vagina Painting* (fig. 4).[8] But this action, criticized by the predominantly male Fluxus milieu and later lauded as a historic feminist act,[9] was just one step in Kubota's dynamic evolution rather than her defining moment. It was when she began experimenting with newly available video technology in the early 1970s that

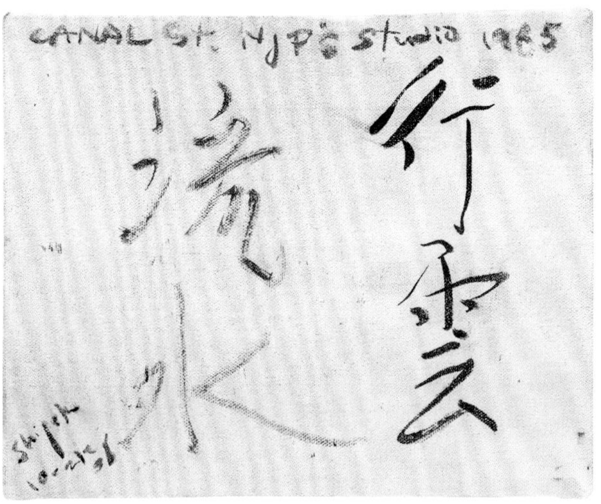

Fig. 2. Untitled. 1965. Acrylic on canvas, 8 × 10 in. (20.3 × 25.4 cm). Shigeko Kubota Video Art Foundation

1 Kubota, in Mary Jane Jacob, ed., *Shigeko Kubota Video Sculpture*, exh. cat. (New York: American Museum of the Moving Image, 1991), 41.

2 Kubota and Paik moved from their apartment in Westbeth Artists Housing, in the West Village, to the loft at 110 Mercer Street in 1974.

3 I am grateful to Dr. Andrew Pekarik for providing the translation for this phrase and sharing his insights on its meaning in the Zen context.

4 Jacob, *Shigeko Kubota Video Sculpture*, 22, 24, 40.

5 Ibid., 35.

6 Kubota and Cage collaborated on a book inspired by *Reunion* (1968), a performance by Cage, Marcel Duchamp, Teeny Duchamp, David Tudor, Gordon Mumma, David Behrman, and Lowell Cross, at the Ryerson Theatre, Toronto, in which electronic music was activated by moves on a modified chessboard. Published in 1969, the book included photographs Kubota took of the performance, which also served as the basis of her video *Marcel Duchamp and John Cage* (1972). Kubota lived at the art colony the Land, in Stony Point, New York, for a time in the early 1970s, overlapping with Cage's time there.

7 Kubota traveled to New York with her friend and fellow artist Mieko Shiomi. Midori Yoshimoto, "Self-Exploration in Multimedia: The Experiments of Shigeko Kubota," in *Into Performance: Japanese Women Artists in New York* (New Brunswick, NJ: Rutgers University Press, 2005), 175.

8 In her early days in New York, Kubota participated in numerous performances, including Carolee Schneemann's *Snows* (1967) and Alison Knowles's *Identical Lunch* (1968–69). She also helped bring the Tokyo-based collective Hi Red Center's *Street Cleaning Event* to New York in 1966.

9 Yoshimoto, "Self-Exploration in Multimedia," 181.

My dear Mr. George Maciunas

Thank you very much for your letter to me again and again.

In every day I was very worry which is better to be in Tokyo or to be in New York in order to live as an only artist.

But Now I made up my mind to go to New York. I'm very sorry to put you to a trouble by my act which is to go to New York.

It's my only hope to go to New York in order to live as a artist, but for you, it's no mean with-out the biggest trouble to You.

But I'd like to touch, to see and to feel something by touching a grop of Fluxus and living by myself in New York.

It's my biggest happening to go to New York "Now, I will not be able to forget to be you in a space of my eternal life.

I will arrive at International (J.F.Kennedy airport) in New York via NW#6 (Northwest orient airlines) At 10:30pm on 20th (saturday) June.

May I be able to meet you at airport?

I'm very sorry to eat your time for me but I'd like to blieve to meet you at airport, availing myself of your kindness.

So, as my mark, I will put on a dress and coat of green color.

1st my mark.

Now I do believe to be able to meet you at airport. but if it's impossible.....

oh. what shall I do!

Best regards to you
See you after few days.

Good-bye

Shigeko Kubota

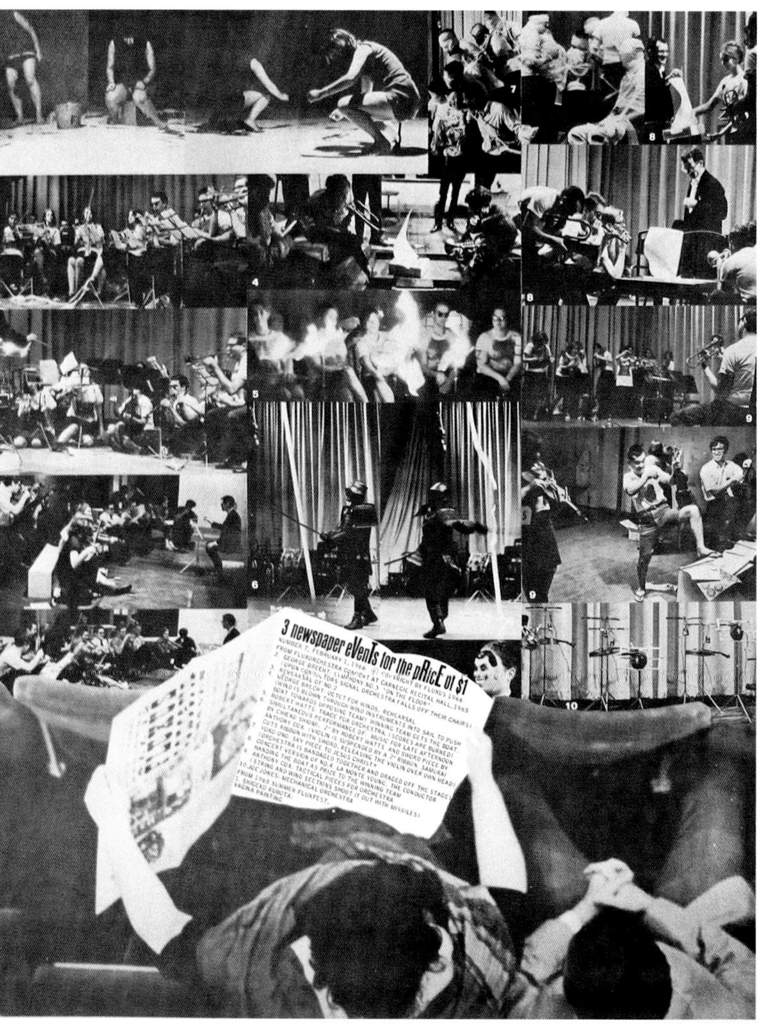

Fig. 3. Letter to George Maciunas. 1964. Ink on paper with collage addition, sheet: 38 ¾ × 11 1⁄16 in. (98.5 × 28.1 cm). The Museum of Modern Art, New York. The Gilbert and Lila Silverman Fluxus Collection Gift, 2008

Fig. 4. George Maciunas. Cover of *Fluxus 3 newspaper eVenTs for the pRicE of $1*, Fluxus newspaper no. 7 (February 1, 1966), showing (at top left) Kubota performing *Vagina Painting* at the Perpetual Fluxfest, New York, July 4, 1965, photographed by Maciunas. Offset lithograph, 21 15⁄16 × 16 15⁄16 in. (55.7 × 43.1 cm). Publisher: Fluxus [New York]. The Museum of Modern Art, New York. The Gilbert and Lila Silverman Fluxus Collection Gift, 2008

she found the kind of freedom "moving clouds, flowing water" might have signified—in the "organic" process of making video images (she later likened Sony's first portable recording and playback system, the Portapak, to a new paintbrush[10]) and in the uncharted territory the nascent medium represented (fig. 5).

Kubota was one of the first artists to commit to video, long before its status as an art form was assured. Along with her adventurous contemporaries, she mined the possibilities of this new medium, which allowed artists to view what they were recording in real time. This transformative capability incited critical investigations of time, the body, language, collectivity, ecology, and the one-way address of television. In parallel, experiments with the manipulation of video's electronic signal revealed its potential as a plastic art form. Kubota moved fluidly between formal and conceptual explorations of the medium, combining them with a fearless interrogation of her own personal, artistic, and cultural identity to crystallize a uniquely expressive vocabulary. Her first experiments with a video camera were manipulated close-up self-portraits, made using the newly invented Paik/Abe Video Synthesizer while she, Paik, and Shuya Abe were teaching at CalArts in 1970–71. Among these tapes was *A Day at the California Institute of the Arts*, which evidence suggests was retitled as *Self-Portrait* and incorporated into the sculptural work *Video Poem* (1970–75) (pages 38–45).[11] From there Kubota quickly pivoted to what would become her signature "video diary" approach, through which she documented personal and artistic journeys, added text or audio commentary, and integrated early image-processing techniques like chroma keying, matting, and colorizing to create a "fusion of video documentary and video art, aiming at the higher dimension of consciousness in style and semantics."[12] Raw and poetic, by turns mundane and profound, this mode of self-reflection was one she sustained throughout her four-decade career in video and, starting in the mid-1980s, conceptualized as an "auto(video)biography" series titled Broken Diary. The series is divided into chapters, the first of which is that early California self-portrait.[13]

For Kubota, video was inseparable from the physical realm from the beginning. Though the Portapak she used was designed to be compact enough to be operated by an individual (older equipment required a crew), it was by no means discreet. The Sony VideoRover II model with which she shot *Europe on ½ Inch a Day* (1972), for example, weighed nearly nineteen pounds including battery pack, tape, and reel. In stark contrast to today's nearly weightless image-making technologies, and the invisible mechanisms with which digital information is recorded and circulated, early analog video equipment had an imposing presence, an unavoidable fact that Kubota chose to emphasize, writing, around 1973, "I like video because it is heavy."[14] She framed the newfound autonomy and

10 "In the 1960s Sony invented the Portapack [*sic*], which was revolutionary; . . . film was chemical, but video was more organic. To me Portapack [*sic*] was like a new paint brush. It was certainly in the same spirit as Fluxus, 'do it yourself.'" Kubota, in "Shigeko Kubota with Phong Bui," *The Brooklyn Rail*, September 2007.

11 Shuya Abe is listed as a collaborating artist on *A Day at the California Institute of the Arts* in David A. Ross, ed., *Southland Video Anthology*, exh. cat. (Long Beach, CA: Long Beach Museum of Art, 1975), n.p. The video is identified as *One Day in California* (1970) in Kubota's grant proposal "Auto(video)biography in Twelve Chapters (1969–86) A Broken Diary" (c. 1986), in the Electronic Arts Intermix Archives, New York. Lori Zippay, "It Rains in My Heart, It Rains on My Video Art," *VoCA Journal*, March 7, 2019. According to Moira Roth, the video was retitled *Self-Portrait*. Roth, "The Voice of Shigeko Kubota: 'A Fusion of Art and Life, Asia and America . . .,'" in Jacob, *Shigeko Kubota Video Sculpture*, 81.

12 Kubota, grant proposal for production of *Video Girls and Video Songs for Navajo Sky* (1973), Shigeko Kubota Video Art Foundation.

13 Circa 1986 Kubota envisioned a cohesive presentation of her twelve Broken Diary works made to date, writing, "This endeavor will also serve, hopefully, as a model for other video makers, professional and amateurs alike, who are hoarding thousands of hours of undigested video plastic memories and are afraid to look back. Some of them may be as valuable as the best chapters of fiction or non-fiction writers." Kubota, "Auto(video)biography in Twelve Chapters."

14 Kubota, "Women's Video in the US and Japan," in *The New Television: A Public/Private Art*, ed. Douglas Davis and Allison Simmons (Cambridge, MA: MIT Press, 1977), 97. This publication was based on "Open Circuits: An International Conference on the Future of Television," which took place at MoMA in 1974. Kubota participated in the opening panel discussion, "Global Trends in Experimental Television," during which she may have presented "Women's Video in the US and Japan." She had conceived the text circa 1973, as she was planning, with Elsa Tambellini, a women's video festival in Tokyo. A draft is reproduced in the present volume, on pages 106–11.

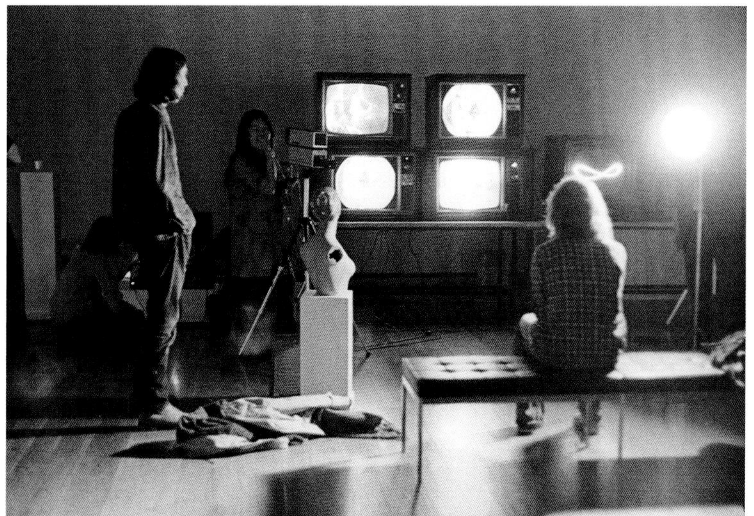

Fig. 5. Kubota using the Paik/Abe Video Synthesizer, installed at the Everson Museum of Art, Syracuse, New York, for the exhibition *Work from the Experimental Television Center*, which included Kubota's work, 1972

15 Kubota, in Chris Meigh-Andrews, *A History of Video Art* (London: Bloomsbury, 2013), 10.
16 Kubota, notes for "Women's Video in the US and Japan," Shigeko Kubota Video Art Foundation.
17 Kubota, in Jacob, *Shigeko Kubota Video Sculpture*, 35.
18 Kubota, in "Shigeko Kubota with Phong Bui." Video itself, in its infinite reproducibility and freedom from precedent, was antithetical to the notions of value prescribed by institutional and commercial frameworks.
19 Kubota's work was first shown at MoMA in 1976, when London included *Video Girls and Video Songs for Navajo Sky* in an earlier Projects exhibition, *Projects: Video VI*; that same year, Kubota's *Video Poem* was included in *Rooms*, the first exhibition at the Institute of Art and Urban Resources (which would become MoMA PS1), organized by Alanna Heiss. At the time *Projects: Shigeko Kubota* took place, the series (founded by Kynaston McShine) was overseen by the curator Riva Castleman; the series continues today.

intense corporeality that characterized early video making in gendered terms: "Portapak and I travelled all over Europe and Japan without male accompaniment. Portapak tears down my backbone, shoulder, and waist. I travel alone with my Portapak on my back, as Vietnamese women do with their babies."[15] Kubota's personification of video technology drives home the extent to which she considered her art and her life to be fundamentally intertwined. She underscored this in her videos (fig. 6) and in her writings, as when she cast herself as a conduit for her medium: "I have a body. I bleed. I am a woman and recently I bleed 3M Scotch tape half-inch—sometimes Sony . . . 2,000 feet a month."[16]

In parallel with her video diaries, in the early 1970s Kubota pioneered yet another medium—video sculpture—by extending her videos into three-dimensional plywood forms, which were constructed by her friend and collaborator the artist Al Robbins. With this gesture Kubota aimed to challenge the widely held notion that the emergent medium of video was "'fragile,' 'superficial,' 'temporal' and 'instant,'"[17] as compared to more established art forms. Her sculptural vocabulary also implicitly pushed against the association of video with corporate technology and mainstream media; "I used plywood to cover the TV box," she explained, "partly because I didn't want people to know what brand the TV was; I just wanted them to see it as sculpture."[18] Her first video sculptures engaged with the work and legacy of Marcel Duchamp, who had become increasingly influential for a younger generation of artists since his death in 1968, and to whom Kubota felt a deeply personal, almost mystical, connection. *Duchampiana: Nude Descending a Staircase* (1976) (pages 46–53), the second work in her series of homages, reimagines Duchamp's oil painting of 1912 through the construction of a physical staircase and the introduction of movement through time and space in the representation of the figure, which is silhouetted, doubled, and rendered in ghostly pixels of brilliant color that simultaneously come together and disintegrate like wet sand. After being shown at The Museum of Modern Art in 1978 in an exhibition organized by the curator Barbara London as part of the Museum's Projects series (established in 1971 to present work by emerging artists)[19] (fig. 7), Kubota's *Nude* was proposed for acquisition by London and entered the collection in 1981 under the auspices of the Department of Painting and Sculpture; as MoMA's first acquisition of a work

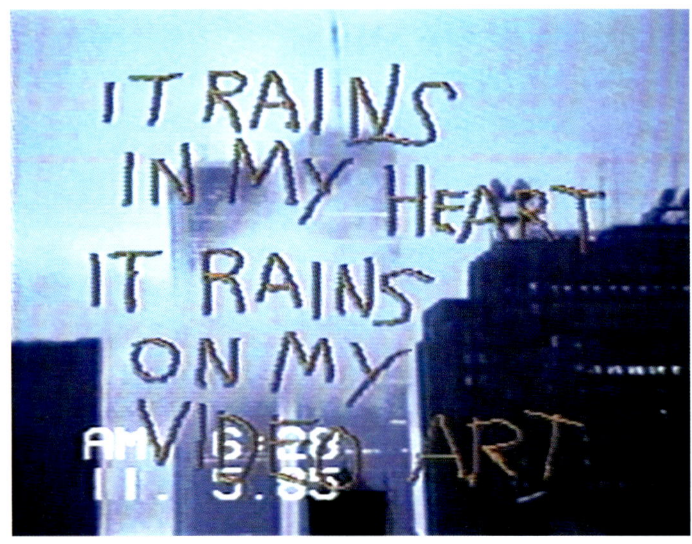

Fig. 6. Still from *SoHo SoAp/Rain Damage*. 1985. Standard-definition video (color, sound), 8:25 min. The Museum of Modern Art, New York. Purchase, 2001

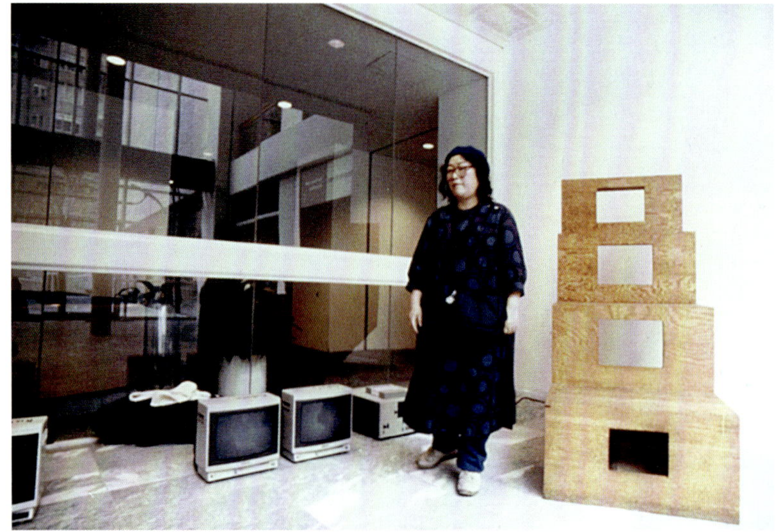

Fig. 7. Kubota with the components of *Duchampiana: Nude Descending a Staircase* (1976) during the installation of *Projects: Shigeko Kubota*, The Museum of Modern Art, New York, 1978

combining video and sculpture, it lay the groundwork for the eventual establishment of a curatorial department and a conservation focus devoted to moving-image-based art beyond film and, ultimately, to live performance as well.[20]

As Kubota's sculptural language evolved, she remained at the vanguard of a generation of artists—referred to by one of them, Jud Yalkut, as "the first Cybernauts"[21]—who sculpted video itself. This practice was deeply collaborative, relying on a network of artists, engineers, and technologists (with significant overlaps between these roles) who designed and administered image-processing tools. A photograph of Kubota creating the video content for her *Meta-Marcel: Window (Flowers)* sculpture while in residence at the Experimental Television Center, in Owego, New York,[22] in 1983 (fig. 8) illustrates how video processing had evolved since she and her peers had first embraced it more than a decade earlier; here, she is seen using multiple live color and black-and-white cameras that were routed to a multichannel Jones Colorizer and other devices, through which she combined and manipulated the footage in real time—"performance time"—and recorded it on tape.[23] This process required both skilled implementation and acceptance of unpredictability; the resulting colors were uncanny, yielding a hyper-saturated palette that had no precedent in any other medium. As the media historian Carolyn Kane has observed, "Herein lies one rationale to understand how electronic color in video synthesis became magical and otherworldly: it literally was."[24]

The preternatural qualities of Kubota's "liquid reality" are particularly striking in her treatment of that which most steadfastly grounds us in what we understand to be real—the prehistoric topography of the earth. In the late 1970s, in parallel with her Duchampiana series, she began making video sculptures that foreground nature through the combination of what she deemed "cool forms"—volumetric objects that echo the contours of mountains, rivers, and waterfalls—with "hot video," in which her imagery of these same features is complicated to varying degrees through colorization, fragmentation, and repetition, or totally deconstructed. In an early preparatory drawing, she labeled her first work of this kind, *Three Mountains* (1976–79) (pages 54–67), an "autobiographical object" that "reflects" her life (fig. 9);[25] writing about it later, she declared, "Sculpture mirrors nature

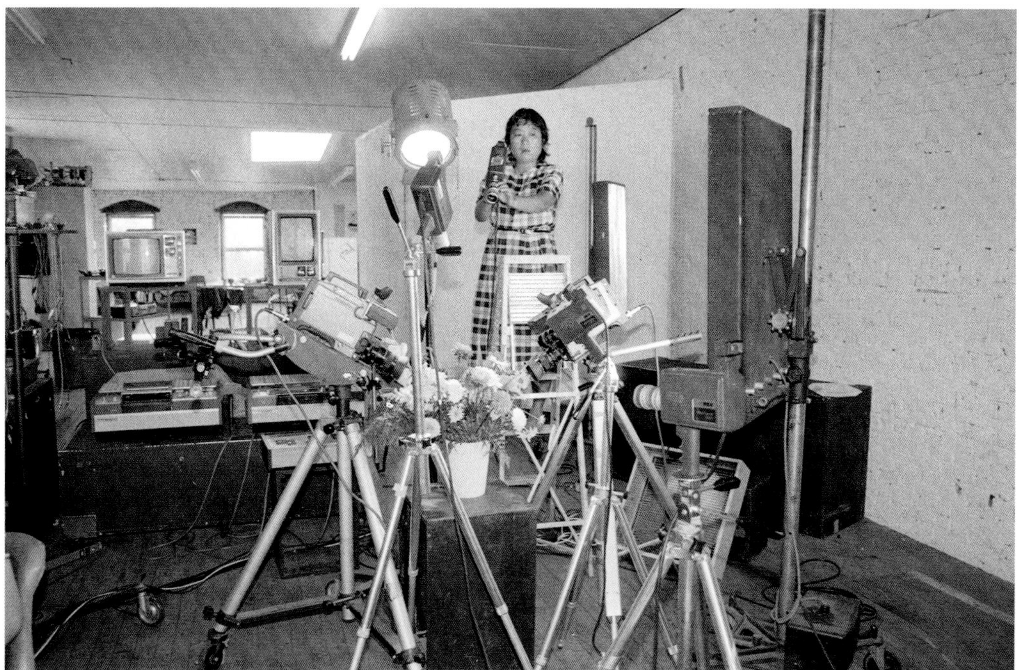

Fig. 8. Kubota shooting footage of flowers for *Meta-Marcel: Window (Flowers)* at the Experimental Television Center, Owego, New York, 1983

20 MoMA's Department of Media was founded in 2006; it became the Department of Media and Performance Art in 2009, and in 2019 its name was adjusted to Department of Media and Performance. The Museum created its first Media Conservator position in 2007.

21 Jud Yalkut, "Electronic Zen: The Alternate Video Generation" (unpublished manuscript, 1984), in the archives of the Experimental Television Center. Examples of early video processing tools include those designed by Paik and Abe, Eric Siegel, Steve Rutt and Bill Etra, Steina and Woody Vasulka, Dan Sandin, Stephen Beck, and David Jones. In addition to the 1972 and 1973 Women's Video Festivals at The Kitchen, Kubota participated in the 2nd International Computer Art Festival there in 1974, alongside Paik, Stan VanDerBeek, the Vasulkas, Etra, and others.

22 The Experimental Television Center, founded in 1971 by the artist Ralph Hocking and directed by Hocking and the artist Sherry Miller Hocking, had moved to Owego from its original home in Binghamton, New York, in 1979. In the 1970s, Kubota also utilized the image-processing equipment at TV Lab, a program founded by David Loxton in 1972 at Thirteen/WNET, a public television station in New York.

23 Peer Bode, email to the author, February 23, 2021. According to Bode, a single "slider matrix" switch in the Experimental Television Center studio would have allowed Kubota to quickly repatch and reprogram the video and signal flow of the studio.

24 Carolyn Kane, "The Electric 'Now Indigo Blue': Synthetic Color and Video Synthesis Circa 1969," *Leonardo* 46, no. 4 (2013): 362.

25 John Hanhardt writes, "This strategic use of the video within the natural form of the mountain becomes a metaphor for the artist in the landscape." Hanhardt, *Shigeko Kubota*, exh. cat. (New York: Whitney Museum of American Art, 1996), 16.

while containing the imprint, the consciousness, of its maker."[26] For Kubota, then, these sculptures were just as personal as her video diaries, the landscape offering a means to contemplate the self: "I walk, I walk, . . . looking for myself," she jotted on a drawing of the desert (page 67), whose "nowhere"-ness had captivated her during her travels out west to shoot the footage for *Three Mountains*. In describing *River*, she wrote, "I'm swimming on the current with the fishes, half being drowned, looking for myself."[27] And the sublime beauty of the eponymous subject of *Niagara Falls I* (1985) (fig. 10; see also pages 84–91) summoned visions of her own death and liberation from the constraints of personhood.[28] The heavily manipulated videos in these works show Kubota searching for a new visual language with which to represent the world and her place in it. Her investigation of what she perceived as a profound synergy between nature and technology, and her understanding of video technology's dual capacity for self-reflection and mediation, are further emphasized in her integration of water, which she used, in addition to mirrors, to reflect and distort video images, themselves always already mediations of "the real."

As her designs for *Three Mountains* evolved, Kubota made a series of revelatory sketches of Land art interventions that she termed "structural video" works, which would have embedded video monitors in the mountain ridges of Arizona and New Mexico, replacing sculptural interpretations of the landscape with the landscape itself. Although her visionary propositions went unrealized, they illustrate what she imagined a complete coalescence of nature and technology might look like, and demonstrate the ambition at the heart of her sculptural practice. "In video, time flows frame by frame," she stated in an interview in 2009. "If I combine it with a still object, the resulting space will be like a museum, like a pantheon. If it is brought to a public space, it can heal people's minds."[29]

26 Kubota, "Mountain Series," in Zdenek Felix, ed., *Shigeko Kubota: Video Sculptures*, exh. cat. (Berlin: Daadgalerie; Essen: Museum Folkwang; Zurich: Kunsthaus Zürich, 1981), 37.

27 Kubota, in Jacob, *Shigeko Kubota Video Sculpture*, 40.

28 Ibid., 55. Emily Watlington argues that Kubota's landscape work "speaks from a subject position while refuting the pigeon-hole of identity politics, situated in a broader desire to obliterate the self." Watlington, "Total Freedom to Dissolve: Shigeko Kubota's Video Sculptures," *Haunt Journal of Art* 4 (October 2017), 11.

29 Kubota, in interview by Tezuka Miwako, October 11, 2009, Oral History Archives of Japanese Art. Translated from the Japanese by Reiko Tomii as "Interview with Shigeko Kubota," *Histories and Theories of Intermedia*, a blog for the University of Maine Intermedia MFA Program, July 27, 2015.

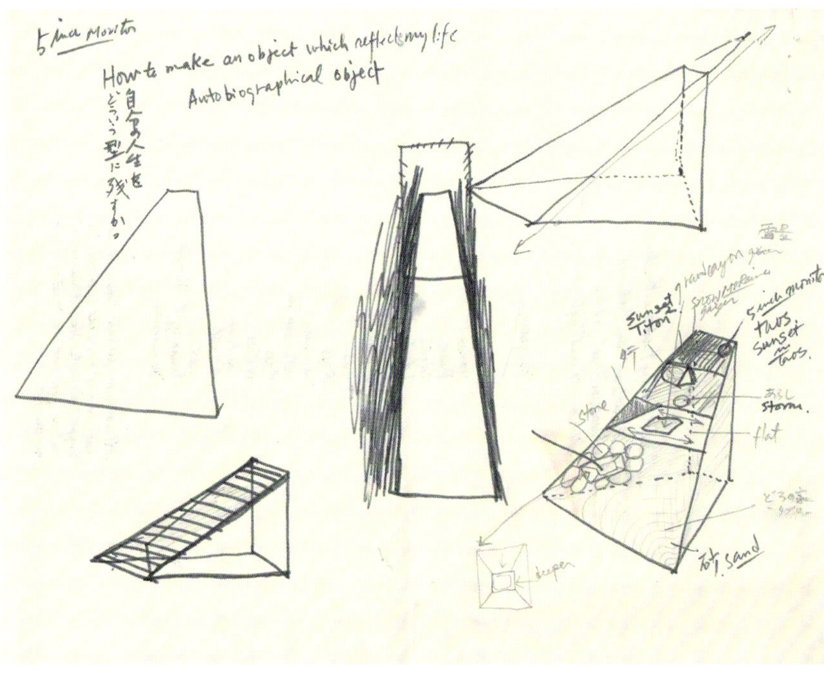

Fig. 9. Sketch for *Three Mountains*. c. 1977–78. Ink on paper, 11 × 14 in. (28 × 35.6 cm). Shigeko Kubota Video Art Foundation

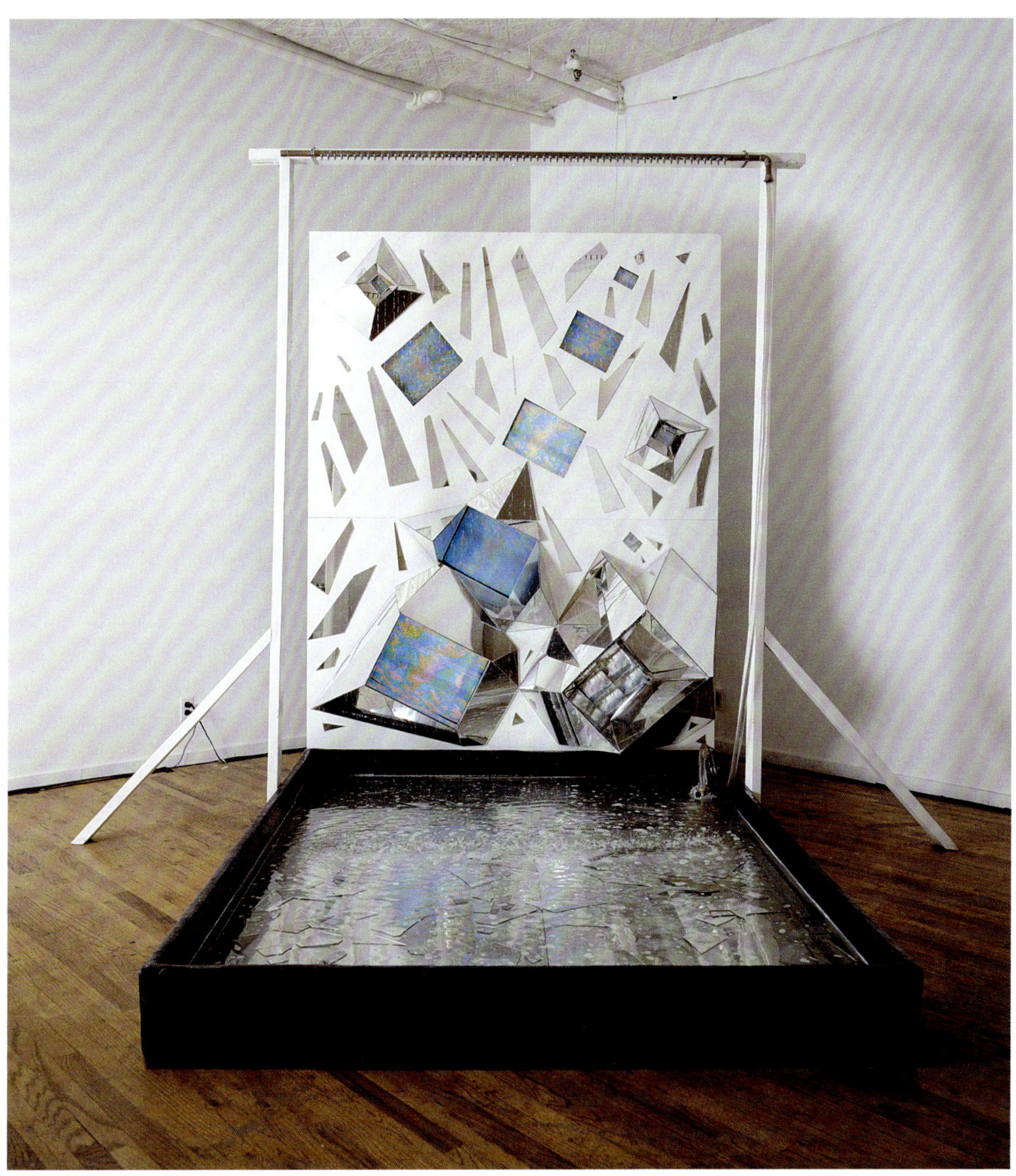

Fig. 10. Peter Moore. Photograph of *Niagara Falls I*. 1985. Four-channel standard-definition video (color, sound; approx. 31 min. each), ten cathode-ray tube monitors, plastic mirrors, plywood, water, and sprinkler system, 8 ft. × 54 in. × 8 ft. (243.8 × 137.2 × 243.8 cm). Shigeko Kubota Video Art Foundation. Installed in *Niagara Falls: Summer, Fall, and Winter*, The Kitchen, New York, March 9–30, 1985

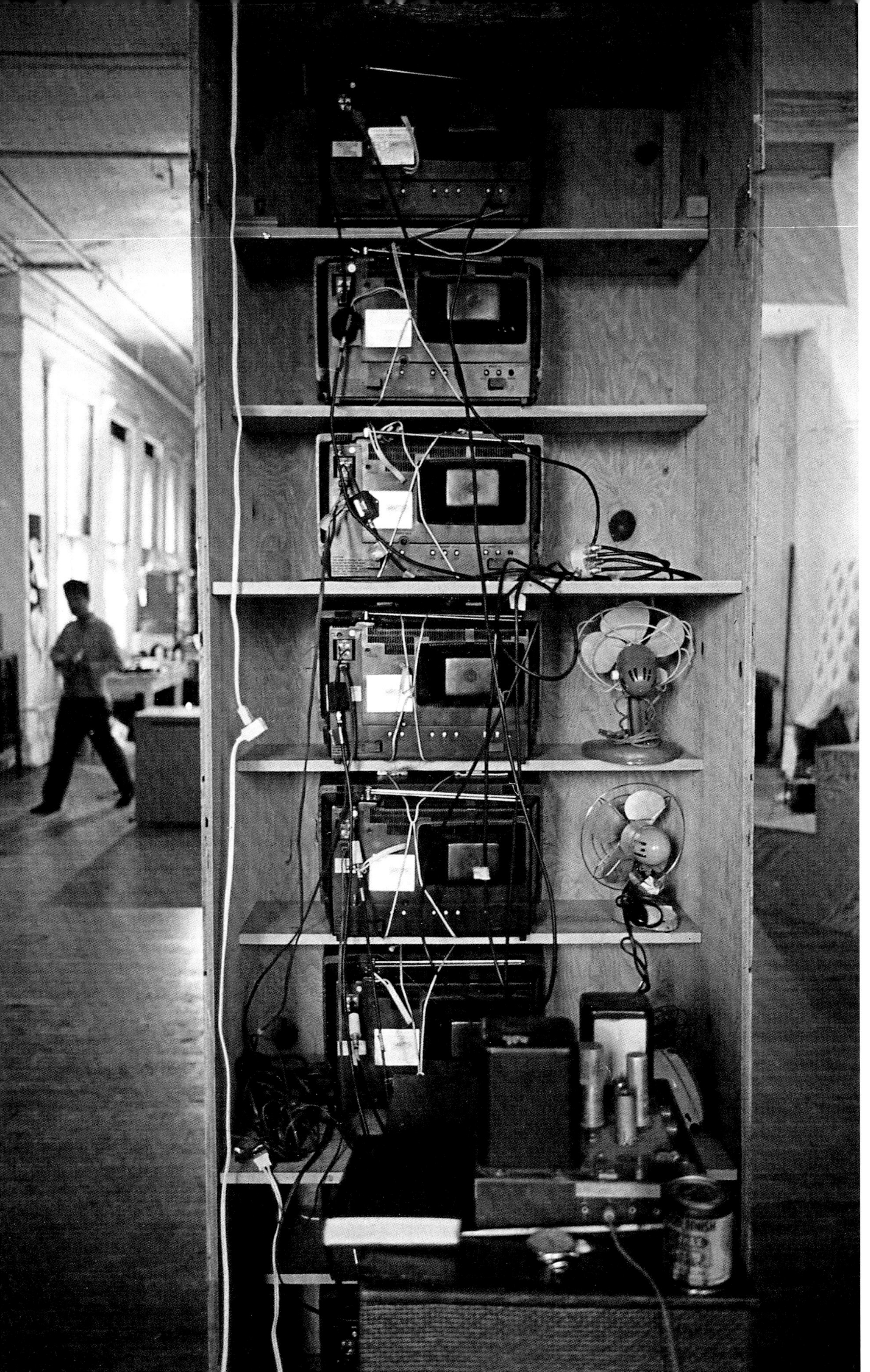

Gloria Sutton

A Matter of Memory: Shigeko Kubota's Video Sculptures

I am a sculptor, I want to make video, but I also wanted to make objects. So the video part is my mirror for my memory, of my life, but the object is creating my creation.

Shigeko Kubota, 1983[1]

The New York–based artist Shigeko Kubota deftly fused video's latent promise of veracity and preservation with its susceptibility to erasure and obsolescence into an art form uniquely her own. Starting in the early 1970s, she interwove video—a signal-based feedback technology comprising portable camera, videotape, playback deck, and monitor—with materials including plywood, sheet metal, and Mylar to generate arresting works that eluded expectations for both sculpture and the nascent field of video art, thus giving viewers, critics, curators, and art historians pause. By embedding time-based media within freestanding architectonic forms, Kubota invited concentrated acts of looking and listening. She determined that moving images could become monuments, and the inverse: inert objects could become animated sites of mediation.

Kubota's inherently hybrid objects mixed disciplinary categories of viewership, combining abstract and minimalist forms, and transgressing the boundaries that separated video sculpture from Minimalist sculpture. The former's promiscuous associations with a global culture industry were set against the latter's concerns with formal purity, despite the fact that practitioners of both of these strains of art making were invested in seriality, iteration, questioning the autonomy of the object, drawing viewers' attention to the edges of a work as a means of framing its context, and, most notably, emphasizing actual (not illusionistic) space. Kubota's video sculptures—her combinatorial proposition—corroborated Donald Judd's famous dictum, issued in his 1965 essay "Specific Objects," that "the best new work in the last few years has been neither painting nor sculpture."[2] While both Kubota's and Judd's rectilinear volumes made signature use of plywood and colored metal sheets and were shown widely from the 1970s to the mid-1990s, when the two artists also resided next door to one another in SoHo, their works rarely intersected in the same exhibitions or art historical accounts. The hybridity of Kubota's video sculptures was at odds with the prevailing monocultural, male-dominated art historical narratives of the period; artworks could be specifically video or sculpture, but not both.

Kubota's combinational proposal can be seen in her merging of natural formations (mountains, rivers, waterfalls, rocks, blossoms, basins) and manmade structures (graves, steps, windows, ramps, pyramids). It is also evident in her frequent intermixing

1 Kubota, in "Shigeko Kubota: An Interview," conducted by Jeanine Mellinger, 1983, Video Data Bank, School of the Art Institute of Chicago.

2 Donald Judd, "Specific Objects," in *Complete Writings 1959–1975* (New York: Judd Foundation, 2015), 181. For a nuanced rereading of "Specific Objects" and contemporary art historical efforts at "debunking" the mythology around Judd and the heroism of Minimalism, see the recording of "Specific Objects: A Donald Judd Symposium, Part 1," organized by The Museum of Modern Art, New York, November 12, 2020, https://www.moma.org/calendar/events/6541.

Peter Moore. Photograph of *Duchampiana: Marcel Duchamp's Grave* (1972–75), seen from the back, in Kubota's loft on Mercer Street, New York, 1975

3 For more on this topic, see Bruce Kurtz, "The Present Tense," in *Video Art: An Anthology*, ed. Ira Schneider, Beryl Korot, and Mary Lucier (New York: Harcourt Brace Jovanovich, 1976), 235. This book, one of the first to contextualize video art and notably edited by artists, includes a contribution by Kubota.

4 Kubota, in Mary Jane Jacob, ed., *Shigeko Kubota Video Sculpture*, exh. cat. (New York: American Museum of the Moving Image, 1991), 32.

5 As Kris Paulsen explains, "Regardless of how we define 'television'—whether we take it to mean networked, distributed video images, or live vision at a distance (tele-vision) as opposed to video's closed circuit and recorded forms," early video remained tied to television by their familial relationship. Paulsen, *Here/There: Telepresence, Touch, and Art at the Interface* (Cambridge, MA: MIT Press, 2017), 52.

of computer-generated graphic sequences with edited footage that memorialized fleeting encounters with family and fellow artists and the varied landscapes she saw during her frequent travels across North and South America, Asia, and Europe. By embedding then state-of-the-art CRT (cathode-ray tube) monitors displaying rapidly shifting images produced by electronic acts of recording, rewinding, fast-forwarding, and freeze-framing within sculptural forms that refer to the deep time of geology in works such as *Three Mountains* (1976–79), *Niagara Falls I–III* (1985–87), and *Rock Video Cherry Blossom* (1986), Kubota mitigated video's association with the futurity of globalization. With this conjunction she foregrounded video's inherent multi-temporality—its reliance on an unsettling provisional present that is stored and replayed over and over.[3] As she asserted in a text that accompanied her *Meta-Marcel: Window* works, the first of which dates from 1976, "Video is the window of yesterday. Video is the window of tomorrow."[4]

Kubota forged a radical commensurability between the subject position addressed by static sculptures and the one addressed by moving images. And she constructed a reciprocal relationship between bodies perambulating around sculptures and the looped playback of women's lived experience, often her own, during a period when these concerns were often seen as mutually exclusive. In broader terms, Kubota's video sculptures positioned signaletic electronic processes alongside social ones, treating diversity and difference—in media, language (written, spoken, and in translation), and gender—not as marginal concerns but as constitutive of the work itself. Her video sculptures provide an impetus to take up video's less discussed technological charge: its role not as an imaging device or a means of visual representation, but as a medium predicated on storing and accessing memories, both personal and social, and on the forces that erode and erase them.

Kubota's video sculptures challenged early video art's preoccupation with transmission and its seemingly intractable association with the aesthetic vocabularies of cinematic projection, the temporal speeds of small-gauge film, and the "liveness" of televisual broadcast.[5] Deviating from both the frontal orientation of the theatrical screen and the cubic encasement of the television set, her works allowed her edited image sequences and synched sounds to spill off the wall into the viewer's arena and to take over entire rooms of galleries and museums. The phosphorescent luminance and rigid tessellated color patterns of her images accentuate early video's aesthetic as distinct from that of film. Instead of refining images by focusing a lens, for example, Kubota often amplified video's reliance on picture rastering, which is determined by the interlacing of scan lines and, just as importantly, the ways these lines often fall out of sync, become smeared due to compatibility issues between international standards, or break down due to the degradation of magnetic video tape.

6 Ina Blom, *The Autobiography of Video: The Life and Times of a Memory Technology* (Berlin: Sternberg, 2016), 160. My essay is indebted to Blom's theorization of early video's material agency as a memory technology.

7 Johannes Gfeller, "Basic Principles of Video Technology," in *Compendium of Image Errors in Analogue Video*, ed. Gfeller, Agathe Jarczyk, and Joanna Phillips (Zurich: Scheidegger and Spiess, 2012), 133.

8 For an analysis of color processes used in early video, see Carolyn Kane, *Chromatic Algorithms: Synthetic Color, Computer Art, and Aesthetics after Code* (Chicago: University of Chicago Press, 2014), 67.

9 Henriette Huldisch, *Before Projection: Video Sculpture 1974–1995*, exh. cat. (Cambridge, MA: MIT List Visual Arts Center; Munich: Hirmer Verlag, 2018), 38. For a nuanced analysis of the ways that museums and international biennials sought to legitimize video art and video projection while simultaneously ignoring if not deriding video sculptures, see ibid., 14–39.

10 My notion of the history of video as a history of marginality came from a generative exchange with Huldisch around her research, which she cites in *Before Projection*, 21. Malin Hedlin Hayden's research demonstrates that women video artists exhibited consistently alongside their male counterparts in the 1970s and '80s, especially relative to women working in painting and sculpture, yet the dominant histories of video art have been unevenly weighted toward the work of the men. See Hayden, *Video Art Historicized: Traditions and Negotiations* (London: Routledge, 2015). Artists born outside the United States who were pivotal to early video art include Jaime Davidovich, Juan Downey, Takahiko Iimura, Marta Minujín, Antoni Muntadas, Paik, Friederike Pezold, and Steina Vasulka.

11 Kubota, in "Shigeko Kubota: An Interview."

Kubota's conception of video as a memory device was informed by the technology's history and ontological drive. Video was invented in 1956 to provide the newly dominant medium of television with the recording memory it did not possess on its own; as the media scholar Ina Blom has theorized, video did so by forming a "new association between recording and watching [that] was premised on the technical properties of videotape as a storage system" rather than as an imaging technology.[6] In its operations, video differs significantly from film, a photographic medium. Whereas 16mm film creates the illusion of movement as its frames advance through a projector at a rate of twenty-four per second, video's movement is not simply determined by the transmission of a set number of pictures per second (twenty-five full frames). It is also dependent on the electrical frequency of transmission, which breaks images down into scan lines that are illuminated by the electron beam of the monitor as the beam (not the image) repeatedly moves horizontally and vertically across the screen. And while, like film, video is considered a moving-image technology, in its analog form it actually relies equally on signaletic pulses of electron beams and on the human eye, which "converts a single dot as it dashes to and fro, into a two dimensional surface."[7] Video's coloration is also contingent upon the perception of individual viewers. Unlike film, whose coloration is based on pigment and is visible on a celluloid strip even without a projection source, video remains colorless (and invisible more generally) until the CRT inside the monitor scans it, revealing a matrix of red, green, and blue microdots—trace points—that coalesce into an "image" in the eye of the viewer only when they step back from the monitor and are able to take in the whole scene.[8]

While the history of early video art may turn on the evolution of signaletic technology and the accessibility of recording and playback equipment, it is also a history of marginality. The medium's predigital aesthetic development was cultivated by so-called alternative art spaces, and when video was shown in museums it was often limited to interstitial areas (stairwells and hallways) and lacked the institutional support, including conservation, afforded painting and sculpture. Video sculpture was often derided for relying on "badly designed" monitors.[9] Most notably, unlike more established mediums, the reception of video as a pluralistic art form in North America was largely shaped by those who prodigiously operated in the margins of American art history: women, immigrants, émigrés, and foreigners.[10] Kubota was all of these.

Born in Niigata, Japan, in 1937, Kubota earned a degree in sculpture in 1960 at the Tokyo University of Education (now University of Tsukuba) (fig. 1).[11] In 1963 she had her first one-person exhibition, at the Naiqua Gallery, in Tokyo, where, according to Kubota, she "piled up fragments of love letters from the floor up to the ceiling of the gallery" and covered

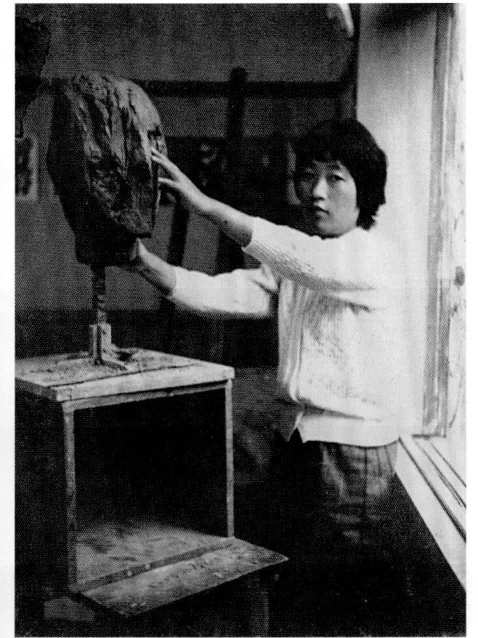

Fig. 1. Kubota in her Tokyo studio with an early sculpture, c. 1962

the stack with a white cloth, creating an unstable mound; "visitors were forced to work their way up the pile of paper scraps" in order to see an array of welded metal sculptures placed at the top (figs. 2, 3).[12] In line with the gallery's role as an oxygenator of the experimental arts in Tokyo, this work was, in the artist's words, "a performance piece that involved audience participation, or was then called 'environmental art.'"[13] Through the gallery Kubota met and collaborated with the avant-garde collectives Hi Red Center, Zero Jigen (Zero Dimension), and Group Ongaku (Music Group), an improvisational music ensemble consisting of Shukou Mizuno and Takehisa Kosugi, whose experiments often included working with dancers, sound, and movement. In fact, in *Video Poem* (1970–75) (pages 38–45), Kubota adapted Kosugi's *Anima 2 (Chamber Music)* (1962), a diaphanous fabric bag he activated in his performance of the same name, to startling effect. Kubota used the bag to encase a monitor playing her *Self-Portrait* (c. 1970–71)—one of the first instances in which she experimented with this type of concealment—so that the haunting colorized image of her face, her mouth wide open but silent (the only sound was the humming of a small fan inside the bag that inflated and rustled the fabric), peeked through a zippered slit, appearing to float like an apparition.

Despite her extensive professional network, which crossed over into the fields of music, film, and dance and put her in contact with Toshi Ichiyanagi, George Maciunas, Yoko Ono, and other international Fluxus figures, Kubota, like many ambitious women artists, realized that gender and social conventions would delimit her opportunities in Japan.[14] "Contrary to my confidence about the [Naiqua Gallery] show and the fact that critics came, no newspapers or art magazines reviewed the show," Kubota later recalled, and she "realized that female artists could not become recognized in Japan."[15] Thus in 1964 she followed the Fluxus network to New York, where she quickly became central to the experimental enterprise that was taking hold downtown, collaborating with Sonic Arts Union (founded by Robert Ashley, David Behrman, Alvin Lucier, and Gordon Mumma) (fig. 4), Allan Kaprow, Ay-O (Takao Iijima), and Nam June Paik while studying at New York University (1965–66), the New School for Social Research (1966–67), and the Brooklyn Museum Art School (1967–68).

Kubota's live-work space in SoHo, which she occupied from 1974 until her death in 2015, was a nexus for emerging and established artists crisscrossing between Europe, Asia, and North and South America, who came to exchange tapes and conversation.[16]

12 Kubota, "Sexual Healing," in *Shigeko Kubota: My Life with Nam June Paik*, exh. cat. (New York: Maya Stendhal Gallery, 2007), 69.

13 Ibid., 70.

14 For a detailed analysis of Kubota's aesthetic development and her influence on other artists, see Midori Yoshimoto, "Self-Exploration in Multimedia: The Experiments of Shigeko Kubota," in *Into Performance: Japanese Women Artists in New York* (New Brunswick, NJ: Rutgers University Press, 2005), 169–93.

15 Kubota, "Sexual Healing," 70.

16 See Barbara London's account of her visits to Kubota's loft. London, *Video Art: The First Fifty Years* (London: Phaidon, 2020), 48–49.

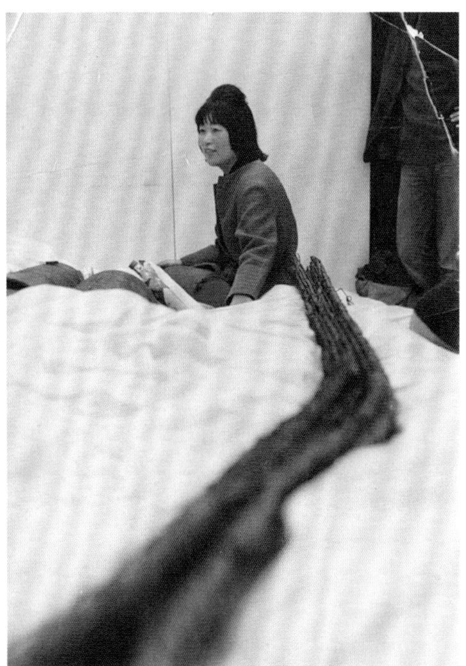

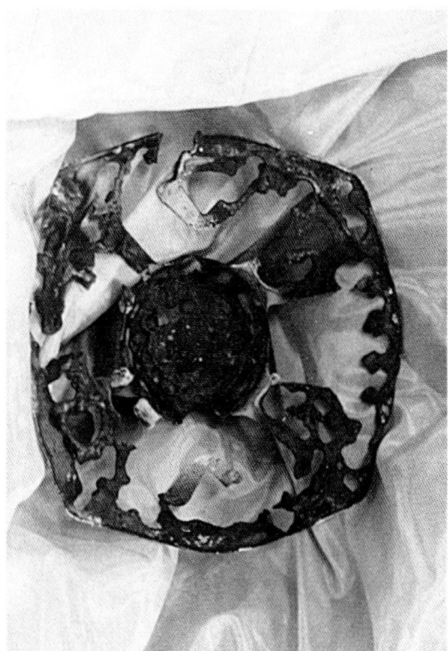

Figs. 2, 3. Kubota with her sculpture *3rd.LOVE* at her exhibition *1st.LOVE, 2nd.LOVE . . .*, Naiqua Gallery, Tokyo, and one of the other sculptures shown, 1963

17 Even after the Fluxhouse Cooperative dissolved, like most utopian projects, due to fiduciary breakdowns and legal problems, the lofts were passed down to other artists. For a detailed history, see Charles R. Simpson, "The Achievement of Territorial Community," *SoHo: The Artist in the City* (Chicago: University of Chicago Press, 1981), 153–88.

18 Kubota, "Anthology Film Archives Video Program: From Film to Video," in *Video Art: An Anthology*, 150.

19 Ibid., 150–55.

Her neighborhood, which only a decade earlier had been known as Hell's Hundred Acres, was at the epicenter of the avant-garde, due in no small part to Maciunas's Fluxhouse Cooperative project. In 1966 he had embarked on an ambitious plan, which drew on his training in architecture and urban planning, to buy underutilized loft buildings, including the one Kubota would eventually reside in, and convert them into collective, affordable live-work spaces. Among those who joined him in the venture were the Film-Makers' Cinematheque and many artists, filmmakers, and scholars, including David Antin, Jonas Mekas, Hollis Frampton, Robert Whitman, and Annette Michelson.[17] Kubota's proximity to these figures, as well as her immediate Mercer Street neighbor Joan Jonas, whose roles in shaping the experimental arts in New York have been well documented, was more than coincidental—it was pivotal. From 1974 to 1982 Kubota was vital in advancing the critical reception of video as a rigorous art form as the first (and only) video curator and woman, and one of the few people of color, associated with Anthology Film Archives, an institution (established in 1970 by Mekas, Jerome Hill, P. Adams Sitney, Peter Kubelka, and Stan Brakhage) that found the variability of video anathema to its Essential Cinema Repertory (figs. 5, 6). Esteemed by peers working in both film and video, Kubota was uniquely positioned to expand "Anthology Film Archives['s] excellent collection and activity to include video and to open its research and performance facilities to video artists."[18] Thus, despite her Japanese origins, Kubota was an influential figure within a specifically American context, working tirelessly to diversify the discourse on film and media and establishing a new, hybrid artist-curator role that would become a mainstay within contemporary art. In fact, her screening and lecture series created some of the few instances when the temple of structural film welcomed projects as diverse as Jon Alpert's decades-long documentary on Cuba and Loren Sears's examinations of Native American medicine, and the work of artists as varied as Stan VanDerBeek, Jackson Mac Low, Douglas Davis, Aldo Tambellini, Ira Schneider, Juan Downey, Takahiko Iimura, and Hans Haacke—associated with divergent artistic praxes including Expanded Cinema, Fluxus, Raindance Corporation and *Radical Software*, performance and Happenings, and the Art Workers' Coalition. Kubota's copiously detailed programming notes for these events traced the formal and conceptual operations of both film and video, considering the two, as the artist-as-curator wrote, "not as mutually competing media, but mutually complementing ones."[19] Additionally, Kubota collaborated with Electronic Arts Intermix (EAI), which was formed in 1971 as one of the

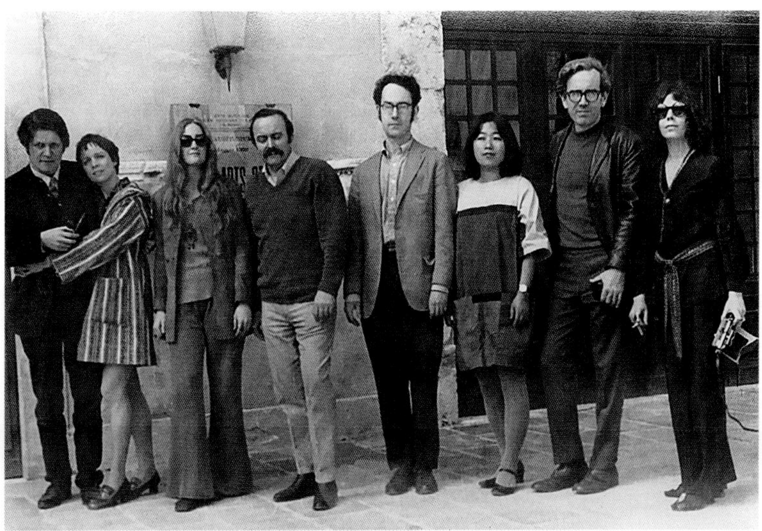

Fig. 4. Sonic Arts Union in L'Aquila, Italy, during a tour, 1969. Left to right: Gordon Mumma, Barbara Dilley, Mary Lucier, Alvin Lucier, David Behrman, Shigeko Kubota, Robert Ashley, and Mary Ashley

first nonprofit organizations to support video as an art form, to present Video Art Reviews at Anthology, further strengthening what Lori Zippay, EAI's director from 1981 to 2019, called the "alternative ecosystem."[20]

In her own practice Kubota purposefully eschewed the emerging vocabularies of projection and performance, which became evocative tools in the hands of Jonas, who wielded mirrors, monitors, video cameras, and a range of props to make associative leaps between the fragmentation of time and space and moments of transformation. Instead, Kubota doubled down on presenting video as sculpture. She explored the possibilities of melding the elemental forms, serial compositions, and industrial fabrication techniques of postwar American sculptural abstraction, for which Judd became the standard, with the developing American feminist engagement with autobiographical video. As the curator JoAnn Hanley suggested in the catalogue for the important 1993 exhibition *The First Generation: Women and Video, 1970–75*, "By turning the camera back on themselves and their daily lives, and by presenting the world from their perspective," women artists bore witness to and validated the complexity of lived experience—especially their own.[21] Kubota's videos, in particular, correspond with what Blom has effectively identified as the "crux of autobiographical video":

The materiality of media time and media memory . . . allows for a pluralizing of subjectivity that complicates its reified or fetishistic dimensions; however minimal, the gap that opens up within the process of producing yourself while seeing yourself in production, also alerts you to the issue of temporalities out of control, a production of existence not already accounted for.[22]

Positioning identities as conditional (as Kubota's uneven art historical reception suggests, one could be read as both a local and a foreigner at the same time), Kubota's video sculptures underscore the ways that feminist artists often used video to open the way to an intersectional view of art. Starting in the 1970s, proponents of both video art and feminism were mutually invested in getting behind the camera in order to challenge the power of authorial mastery. Their primary tactic was the contestation of visual art's established aesthetic conventions, which meant reveling in the mutability—rather than the specificity—of mediums and working against the dominant, commercially driven expectations for image refinement, sound synchrony, and material stability.[23] Kubota achieved this by accentuating the format's glitches, tape misalignments, loss of color lock, and incompatibility issues between television standards (PAL, SECAM, NTSC).

20 See "EAI Oral History: Lori Zippay Interview with Alex Klein and Rebecca Cleman," in *Broadcasting: EAI at ICA*, ed. Rebecca Cleman and Alex Klein (Philadelphia: Institute of Contemporary Art; New York: Electronic Arts Intermix, forthcoming).

21 JoAnn Hanley, *The First Generation: Women and Video, 1970–75*, exh. cat. (New York: Independent Curators Incorporated, 1993), 14.

22 Blom, *The Autobiography of Video*, 36.

23 According to Gabriela Aceves Sepúlveda, this quality is what attracted Mexico City–based artist Pola Weiss to Kubota, whom she interviewed in 1975, and their subsequent epistolary and videotaped exchanges convey a shared investment in developing "an embodied relation with video that empowered their positions as female video producers." See Aceves Sepúlveda, "POLArizing the Archive," in *Women Made Visible: Feminist Art and Media in Post-1968 Mexico City* (Lincoln, NE: University of Nebraska Press, 2019), 260.

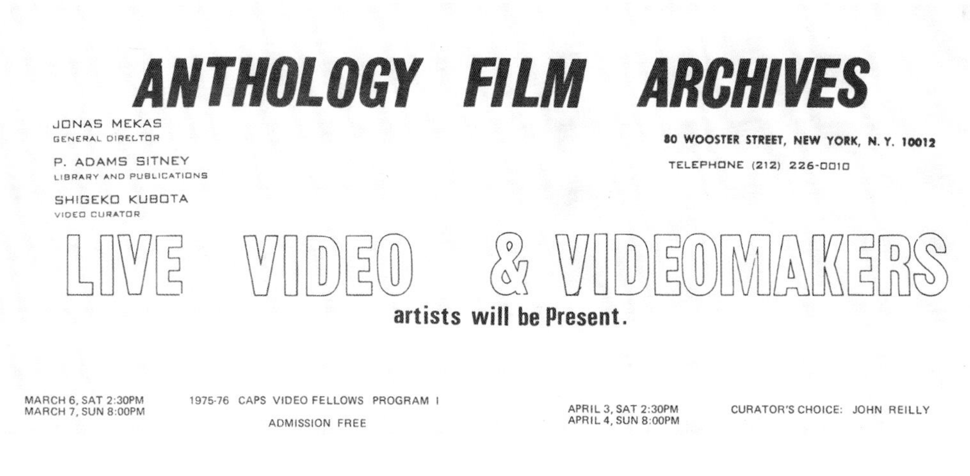

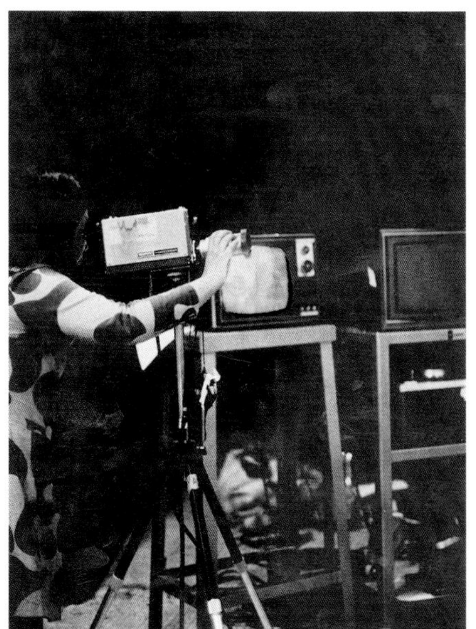

Fig. 5. Detail from the program for the "Live Video & Videomakers" screening series at Anthology Film Archives, New York, March 6–April 25, 1976

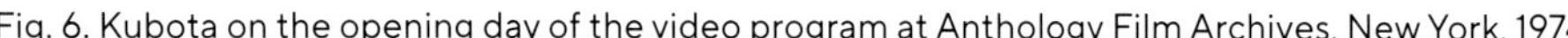

Fig. 6. Kubota on the opening day of the video program at Anthology Film Archives, New York, 1974

24 Kubota, in Jacob, *Shigeko Kubota Video Sculpture*, 24. For an analysis of video as an extension of the Duchampian readymade, see David Joselit, "No Exit: Video and the Readymade," *October*, no. 119 (Winter 2007): 37–45.

25 Kubota, in "Shigeko Kubota: An Interview."

For Kubota, undoing notions of mastery also meant juxtaposing the iterative nature of time-based media with the cyclical patterning of life itself, as seen especially in her early video sculptures, which foreground mortality and contingency. She relied on the intimacy of proximity to articulate the very human desire for companionship and the embodied experiences of aging, disability, grief, and loss. In its fragility, memory is conveyed as a limitation both for human beings and for the medium of video, destined to fade and die out. "Video without Video / Communication with Death," she wrote in relation to the early video sculpture *Duchampiana: Marcel Duchamp's Grave* (1972–75) (figs. 7, 8), one of a series (titled Duchampiana) of homages to the artist whose concept of the readymade loomed large not only in Kubota's intellectual formation but in video's critical stance toward subjectivity as a whole.[24] Kubota referred to this work as a "mental landscape," and its muted video imagery blurs the memory of Duchamp as well as her trip to Rouen to find his grave.[25] Scaled to fit the height of the exhibition space (the first being The Kitchen, in 1975), *Marcel Duchamp's Grave* features a variable number of nine-inch monitors stacked on top of one another inside a plywood column, with just their screens visible through evenly spaced square cutouts. Initially a fourteen-inch-wide mirrored plank was positioned on the floor, perpendicular to the column; in 1984 another mirrored plank, of the same width and length, was mounted on the ceiling, extending the continuous line

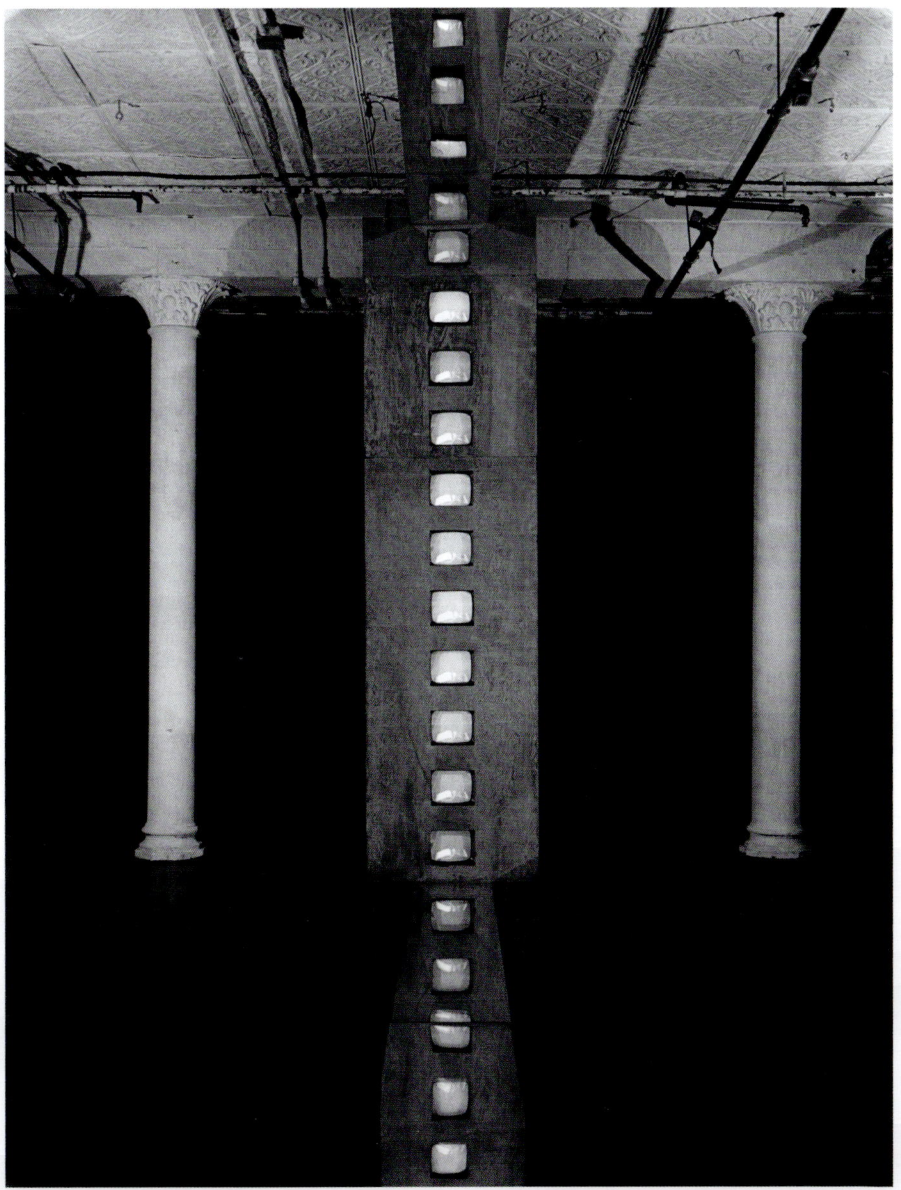

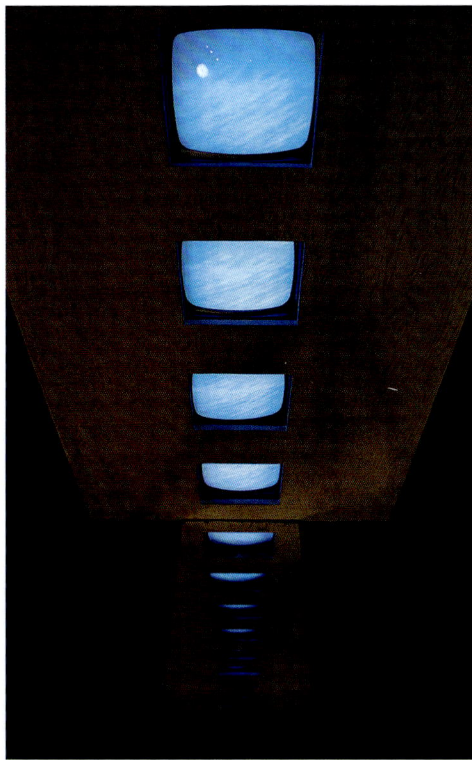

Fig. 7. Peter Moore. Photograph of *Duchampiana: Marcel Duchamp's Grave*. 1972–75. Video (black and white and color, sound; 14:15 min.), eleven monitors, plywood, and mirrors, overall dimensions variable, plywood column: 36 in. (91.4 cm) wide. Shigeko Kubota Video Art Foundation. Installed in *Marcel Duchamp's Grave (Revived)*, The Kitchen, New York, December 18–29, 1984

Fig. 8. Peter Moore. Photograph of *Duchampiana: Marcel Duchamp's Grave* (detail). 1972–75. Installed in *3 Video Installations: Duchampiana*, René Block Gallery, New York, January 24–February 17, 1976

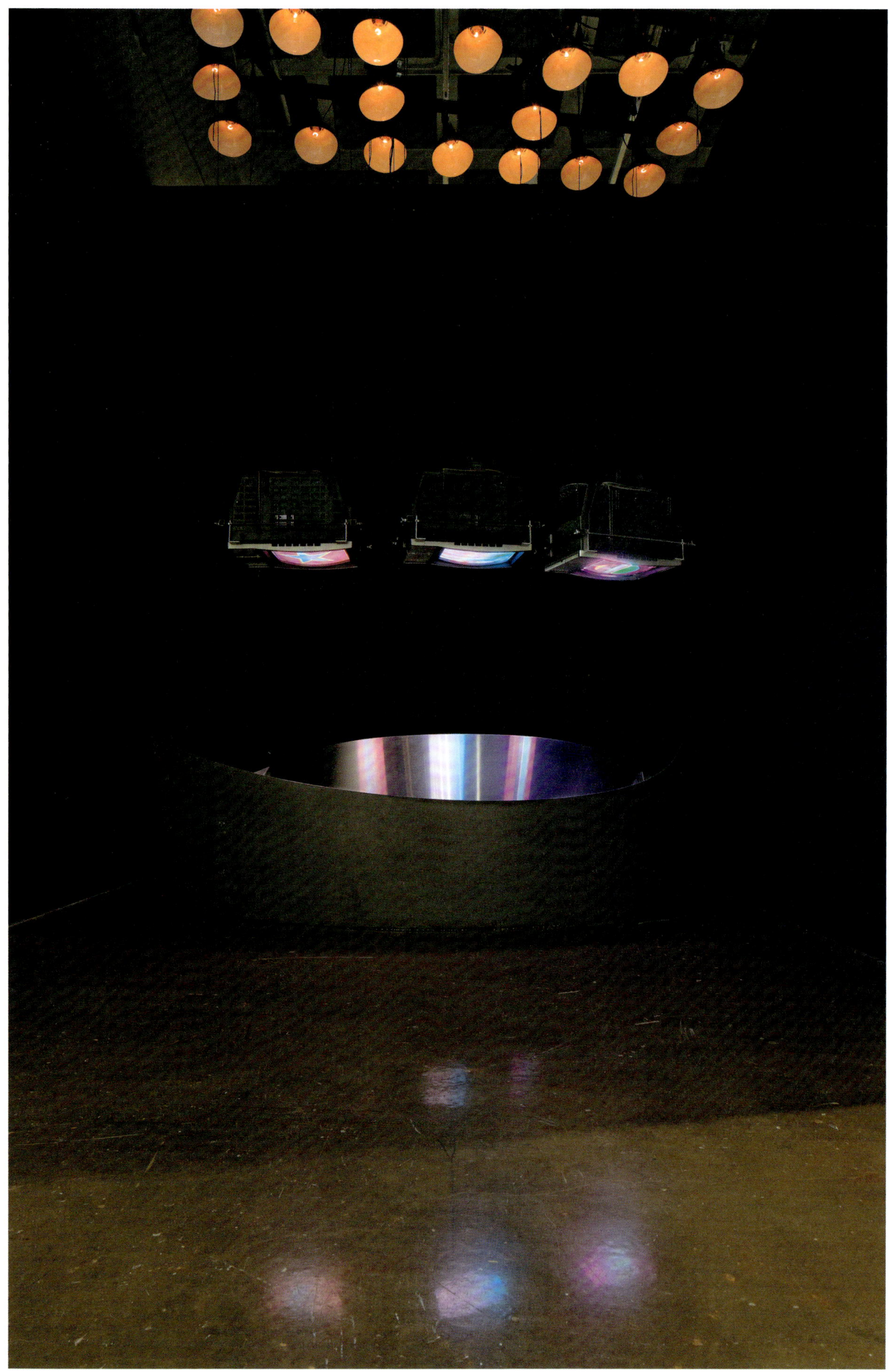

26 Kubota, "Video Sculpture: Two Phases," in Zdenek Felix, ed., *Shigeko Kubota: Video Sculptures*, exh. cat. (Berlin: Daadgalerie; Essen: Museum Folkwang; Zurich: Kunsthaus Zürich, 1981), 19. Translation by the author.

27 John Hanhardt, "Video/Television Space," in *Video Art: An Anthology*, 224.

28 Hanhardt, "Shigeko Kubota: Sculptural Surfaces/ Video Spaces," in *Shigeko Kubota*, exh. cat. (New York: Whitney Museum of American Art, 1996), 12.

of the monitors and their reflections. Simultaneously towering over the viewer and running across the floor, the glowing images illuminate the darkened and otherwise empty space in which the work is installed. Colorized footage Kubota shot roaming the Cimetière Monumental and close-ups of Duchamp's ledger stone solemnly float in washes of saturated color. She described the experience: "Alone, after a long search in the vast cemetery, the weight of my porta-pack crushing on my shoulder, I finally found Duchamp's grave next to that of Jacques Villon, his brother. Marcel's ironic epitaph surprised me . . . 'D'ailleurs, c'est toujours les autres qui meurt [*sic*]' [By the way, it is always others who die]."[26] However, the diminutive size of the screens thwarts efforts to focus on a single monitor or the narrative content. Instead, as the curator John Hanhardt observed firsthand, "the images dissolve into a matrix of weaving colors, camera movements, and recognizable patterns. . . . In a sense one is experiencing the video as a sculpture/collage whose effectiveness is achieved through an abstraction of image and of the video screen."[27] As a result, *Marcel Duchamp's Grave* is less a portrait of Duchamp or a record of Kubota's visit to France than an open circuit or a variable loop that physically refracts and abstracts the video imagery, like an unstable memory.

The multiplication of images via reflective surfaces would become a hallmark of Kubota's video sculptures. In *River* (1979–81) (fig. 9; see also pages 68–77), for example, three monitors are elegantly suspended from the ceiling, the dense black boxes transformed into a single floating line, their bulky weight seemingly, and improbably, held up by the thin black electrical wires that obscure the steel cables actually doing the heavy lifting. Rather than turning out toward the viewer, the monitors' screens face down directly over a crescent-shaped stainless-steel basin filled with water, its bottom scattered with small square mirrors that reflect the videos. The undulating surface of the water softens and naturalizes the images—Kubota swimming in Wyoming's Snake River, feedback static, hard-edged zigzags, pulsating stars, and hearts—all rendered in brilliant synthetic colorized geometric ripples, a result of early video's reliance on composite signals that run along horizontal and vertical axes. The orientation of the monitors denies the primacy of the monitor's screen, offering a less stable image surface that continually coalesces and breaks apart as the water shifts. *River* harks back to Kubota's earliest paintings and sculptures, for which she gained national recognition in Japan in 1954 (fig. 10). Those works, which evoke flowers and water, negotiate between figuration and abstraction, the metaphorical and the personal.[28] In a text about *River*, Kubota drew connections between water and video:

Fig. 9. *River*. 1979–81. Three-channel standard-definition video (color, silent; approx. 32 min. each), three cathode-ray tube monitors, stainless steel, plastic mirrors, water, and wave machine, overall dimensions variable, basin: 22 × 9 × 4 ft. (670.6 × 274.3 × 121.9 cm). Shigeko Kubota Video Art Foundation. Installed in *Before Projection: Video Sculpture 1974–1995*, MIT List Visual Arts Center, Cambridge, Massachusetts, February 8–April 15, 2018

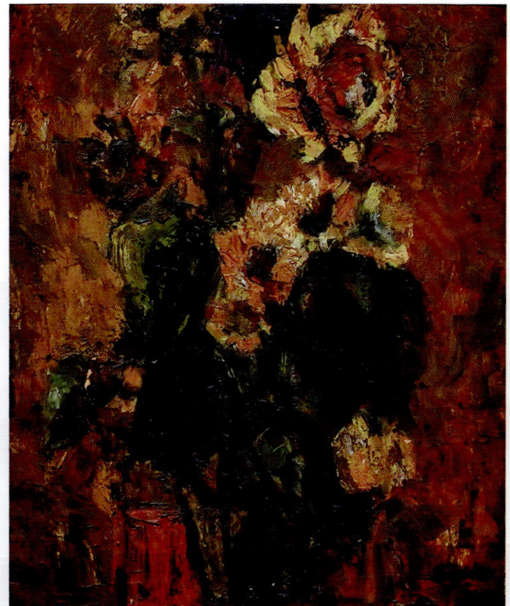

Fig. 10. *Sunflower*. 1954. Oil on canvas, 28 9/16 × 23 13/16 in. (72.5 × 60.5 cm). Private collection

A river is replicated in video in its physical/temporal properties and in its information-carrying and reflective, 'mirror' qualities. . . . Rivers connected communities separated by great distances, spreading information faster than any other means. . . . Charged electrons flow across our receiver screens like drops of water, laden with information carried from some previous time (be it years or nanoseconds).[29]

As her preparatory sketches and notes for *River*, as well as those for *Three Mountains* and *Niagara Falls I*, confirm, Kubota considered the formal properties of video as malleable as those of ink washes and line drawings. Having worked in video since its inception as an art form, she had the technical skills to add texture and depth to her tapes by editing them on playback decks, incorporating computer-generated graphics, overlaying subtitles, and synching sound. Additionally, Kubota was constantly iterating her own work, often reediting footage that was personally significant and producing new sequences. As Hanley noted, "Through video, Kubota's past—images out of memory—is reborn. Restructured, reinterpreted, reviewed, and reorganized, favorite passages appear like old friends, recognizable despite the changes wrought by time and experience."[30] Key to her ability to capture raw footage was the relative mobility afforded by the Sony Portapak, which she acquired in 1970, a few years after it appeared on the market, and constantly carried with her to record both the mundane and epiphanic encounters in her life. Kubota edited her recordings into a remarkable series of single-channel videos, or "chapters," collectively called Broken Diary.[31] *Europe on ½ Inch a Day* (1972), one such chapter, its title a play on the popular guidebook *Europe on Five Dollars a Day*, offers a realistic view of the complications of budget travel, for women in particular, meant to counter the gloss of many travel books. Other chapters attempt to articulate more internalized or subjective states, such as *My Father* (1973–75) (fig. 11), which grapples with the incalculable suffering caused by her father's death and her inability to be present for it. In a tightly framed shot, Kubota cries and touches a television screen on which plays footage she had shot a year earlier of her father lying in bed ill with cancer, as they watched a televised pop music concert together. Showing the artist mourning remotely via video, *My Father* is both a proxy for and a record of grief. Text overlays transmit her lament at having bought her airplane ticket too late to say goodbye or attend his funeral in Japan, and the melodramatic voices of the female singers, often seen in close-up, blare in the background of both recordings, further distorting what is past and what is present.

While the advent of the Portapak ushered in video art's enduring rhetoric of ease and portability, the on-the-ground reality was often quite difficult: "When I began taking

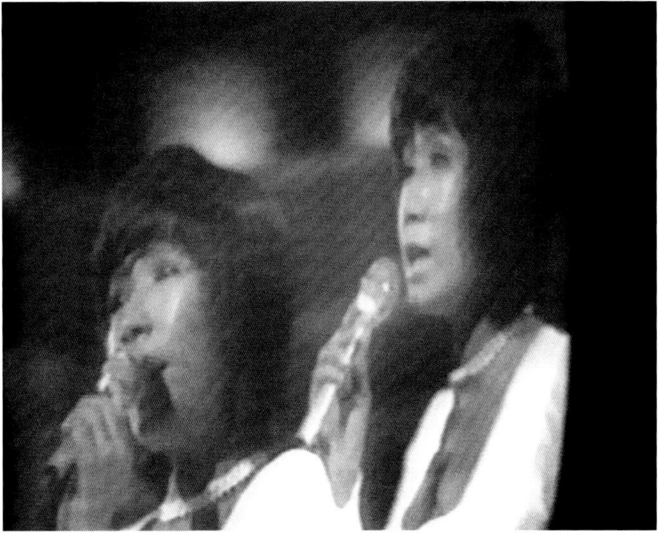

Fig. 11. Still from *My Father*. 1973–75. Standard-definition video (black and white, sound), 15:30 min. The Museum of Modern Art, New York. Purchase, 2001

29 Kubota, in Jacob, *Shigeko Kubota Video Sculpture*, 40–41.
30 Hanley, "Reflections in a Video Mirror," in Jacob, *Shigeko Kubota Video Sculpture*, 88.
31 For a close reading and contextual account of Broken Diary, see Lori Zippay, "It Rains in My Heart, It Rains on My Video Art," *VoCA Journal*, March 7, 2019. The Shigeko Kubota Video Art Foundation recently uncovered previously unseen materials from the artist's Broken Diary series among the approximately two thousand tapes and open reels (unformatted analog video) that compose her video library.

38 Ibid., 37.
39 Ibid.

Montana, Wyoming, Utah, Arizona, and New Mexico in vibrant color video, often from the window of her moving car (and at least once from a helicopter). Kubota edited the sequences and inserted tessellated patterns over them. She then embedded these videos in her watershed video sculpture *Three Mountains* (pages 54–67). Specifically, each five- or thirteen-inch CRT monitor is recessed in a trapezoidal void cut into a plywood form and surrounded by adjoining panels lined with mirrors that reflect and multiply the distinctive desert landscape that flashes onscreen, the extreme rock outcroppings and cloud formations further dramatized by Kubota's fluorescent colorization, color smearing, and accentuation of hue errors endemic to video. A hidden speaker plays audio of rushing wind and other ambient sounds recorded by Kubota during the trip, while the typed text "Why is Arizona so dry?" scrolls horizontally across the screen like a news feed. *Three Mountains* marked the artist's move away from her earlier Duchampian references and continued her exploration of memory processes in relation to video—both in its technological imperative to store and access recorded events and in its self-reflexive connection to autobiography—underscoring that both the medium and subjectivity are always variable, contingent, and subject to the vagaries of time. "People wonder why I am making mountains," she wrote before asking, rhetorically, "'Why do I climb the mountain?' Not, 'Because it is there,' a colonialist/imperialist notion,' but, to *perceive*: to *see*. The mountains provide a visual storm of perceptual complexity in a setting of almost incomprehensible mass and volume."[38] Kubota could have been referring both to her direct experience driving through the American West and to the resulting doubly moving images (shot while in motion and also sped up and slowed down at different moments in the edited sequences). (The vibrant images seem to waver in space due to the mirrors, which themselves perceptually shift between two and three dimensions. Kubota placed actual rocks in the first version of this work, accentuating the play between 2D images and 3D form (fig. 13). (The relationship between 3D forms and flat surfaces continued to inform Kubota's thinking, as evidenced by an assemblage related to this work that she made in 1979 [fig. 14]). The result is that *Three Mountains*, like many of her video sculptures, exists in what Kubota described as "fractured and distended time and space. My vanishing point is reversed, located behind your brain. Then, distorted by mirrors and angles, it vanishes in many points at once. Lines of perspective stretch on and on, crossing at steep angles, sharp like cold, thin mountain air. Time flies and sits still, no contradiction."[39]

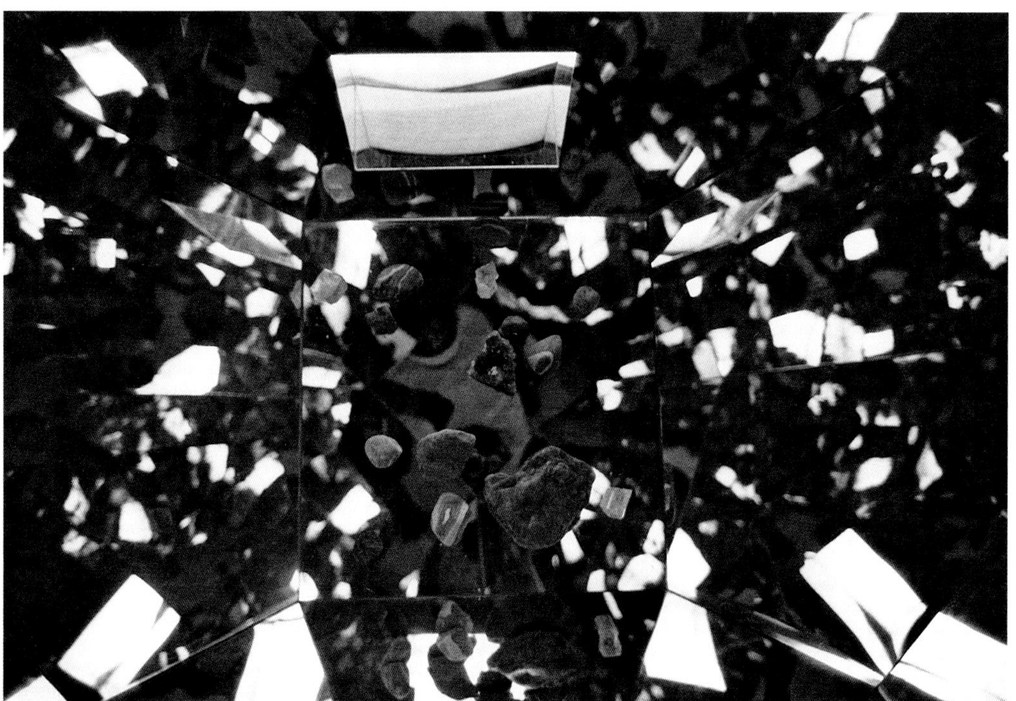

Fig. 13. Peter Moore. Photograph of *Mountain* (detail), the first version of *Three Mountains* (1976–79). Installed in *Meta-Marcel*, René Block Gallery, New York, January 22–March 5, 1977

in *Marcel Duchamp's Grave*. The CCTV techniques Kubota foregrounded in *Video Haiku* found greater currency in not only Paik's work but also that of Bruce Nauman and many other artists who were Kubota's peers and who would be credited more than her with advancing video as an art form.[43] Despite being marginalized by art history, Kubota proved to be an indefatigable force—as an artist as well as a critic, a curator, and a collaborator who undeniably shaped video from these distinct vantage points.

During her first decade in New York, at the same time that she was studying, managing Fluxus events (Maciunas referred to her as the vice president of Fluxus), and exhibiting internationally, Kubota also worked as a New York–based international critic for the Japanese art magazine *Bijutsu techo* (Art handbook). With her knowledge and expertise as an artist, she was one of the few critics able to write fluently on subjects as diverse as music, dance, poetry, film, and electronic media. A six-page article by Kubota (which included her own color images) (fig. 15) introduced Japanese audiences to the landmark 1969 Howard Wise Gallery exhibition *TV as a Creative Medium*, which, as the critic Marita Sturken wrote in 1984, "effectively pointed to the diverse potential of a new art form and social tool" and inspired a generation of artists to take up video as a form of art and activism.[44] The show went largely ignored by US publications, but it prompted Kubota to provocatively raise an issue that would subsequently undergird discussions about how media technology impacts the dispersion of images:

> *It's often said that in contemporary and future society the transmission and circulation of artworks will be valued more than their production. In such a society, where the "original" is hardly ever accessible, this raises the question about the relevance of and reliance on heliotypes. Through the rise of VTR and broadcast satellites, perhaps the "original" artwork may become less important than the ability for that work to be electronically circulated with ease.*[45]

Kubota's investment in fostering artistic dialogue across linguistic, geographical, and gender divides led her to develop peer-to-peer networks for exchanging tapes. She worked tirelessly to advance the work of women, and in her essay "Women's Video in the US and Japan," published in 1977, she argued, "It is important to note that the success of video movement (male and female) is in large part due to the hidden devotion of such woman organizers as Phyllis Gurshuny and Beryl Korot of Radical Software or Dorothy Chiesa and Olivia Tappan of WGBH, Boston, who have worked hard with little material reward."[46] This commitment to using her visibility to foreground others figured into the way she curated the signal 1974 exhibition *Tokyo–New York Video Express* (fig. 16). Just ten

43 While Nauman's CCTV experiments predate Kubota's, focusing on firsts as best reinforces a paternalistic lineage that Kubota seemed determined to break. For a feminist reading of Nauman's early video installations set against Stuart Hall's discourse of encoding and decoding meaning, see Gloria Sutton, "Reciprocal Experience: Decoding Bruce Nauman's Spatio-Temporal Installations," in *Bruce Nauman: A Contemporary*, ed. Eva Ehninger and Martina Venanzoni (Basel: Laurenz Foundation and the Schaulager, 2018), 87–113.

44 Marita Sturken, "TV as a Creative Medium: Howard Wise and Video Art," *Afterimage*, May 1984, 5. Wise closed his gallery in 1970 to focus on setting up Electronic Arts Intermix. Kubota was part of the original cohort of artists the nonprofit would support.

45 Kubota, "TV as a Creative Medium," *Bijutsu techo* 317 (September 1969): page 175. Translation from the Japanese provided by Lia Robinson, Shigeko Kubota Video Art Foundation. Heliotypes are photomechanically produced plates, i.e., materials considered to be original image sources.

46 Kubota, "Women's Video in the US and Japan," in *The New Television: A Public/Private Art*, ed. Douglas Davis and Allison Simmons (Cambridge, MA: MIT Press, 1977), 100.

47 Ibid., 100.

48 According to Lucier, it was Kubota who wanted to foreground their racial identities. Lucier, "Sun Cycles," interview by Tanya Zimbardo, *VoCA Journal*, March 7, 2019. For a compelling account of the limited extant documentation of this project, see Melinda Barlow, "Red, White, Yellow and Black: Women, Multiculturalism and Video History," *Quarterly Review of Film and Video* 17, no. 4 (2000): 297–316.

years after she had left Tokyo in frustration over the lack of recognition afforded women artists, she returned to introduce a Japanese audience to the work of many women video artists, including Mako Idemitsu and Kyoko Michishita, who were part of the Tokyo-based collective Video Hiroba. "Alternating between Japanese and American videotapes," Kubota later reflected, "we achieved not vertical communication from top to bottom, but lateral communication from friend to friend."[47] This horizontal model was also visible in Kubota's feminist collaboration with the artists Mary Lucier and Cecilia Sandoval and the poet Charlotte Warren, which they sometimes called White Black Red & Yellow to foreground its multiracial composition, and at other times Red White Yellow & Black as a play on the "red, white, and blue" of the American flag.[48] This intentional slippage accentuated the strictures of racial categorizations and single authorship while conveying the loose nature of their avant-garde ensemble, which came together for just three "multimedia concerts" at The Kitchen in winter 1972 and spring 1973. The poster for one of these events features each member in stark profile, conveying a sense of activist solidarity and feminist criminality, a reflection of their transgressions against multiple conventions (fig. 17). Though short-lived, their collaboration merged the agit prop and critical strategies of video, theater, and poetry to convey a decidedly intersectional view of identity, one that allowed them to stand together as feminists while standing apart, marked by the complexities of their own lived experiences.

In 1991 the American Museum of the Moving Image, in New York, presented a nearly thirty-year survey of Kubota's work. According to the artist, this show was first slated for the New Museum, also in New York, under the auspices of the curator William Olander, who had worked with her in 1985 when he organized an exhibition featuring the New York Foundation for the Arts Video Fellows, which included Kubota as well as Tony Oursler, Martha Rosler, and Dee Dee Halleck (founder of the nonprofit public-access television program and collective Paper Tiger TV)—a full cross section of video as contemporary art. Olander's death at the age of thirty-eight from HIV/AIDS in 1989 halted Kubota's survey. And though the curator JoAnn Hanley was tapped to guest curate and an Andy Warhol

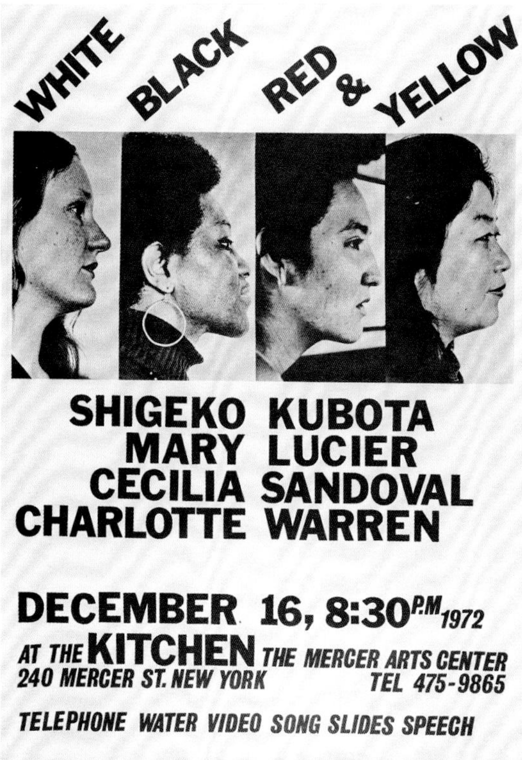

Fig. 17. Poster for a White Black Red & Yellow event at The Kitchen, New York, December 16, 1972, during which Kubota presented her video installation *Riverrun—Video Water Poem* (1972)

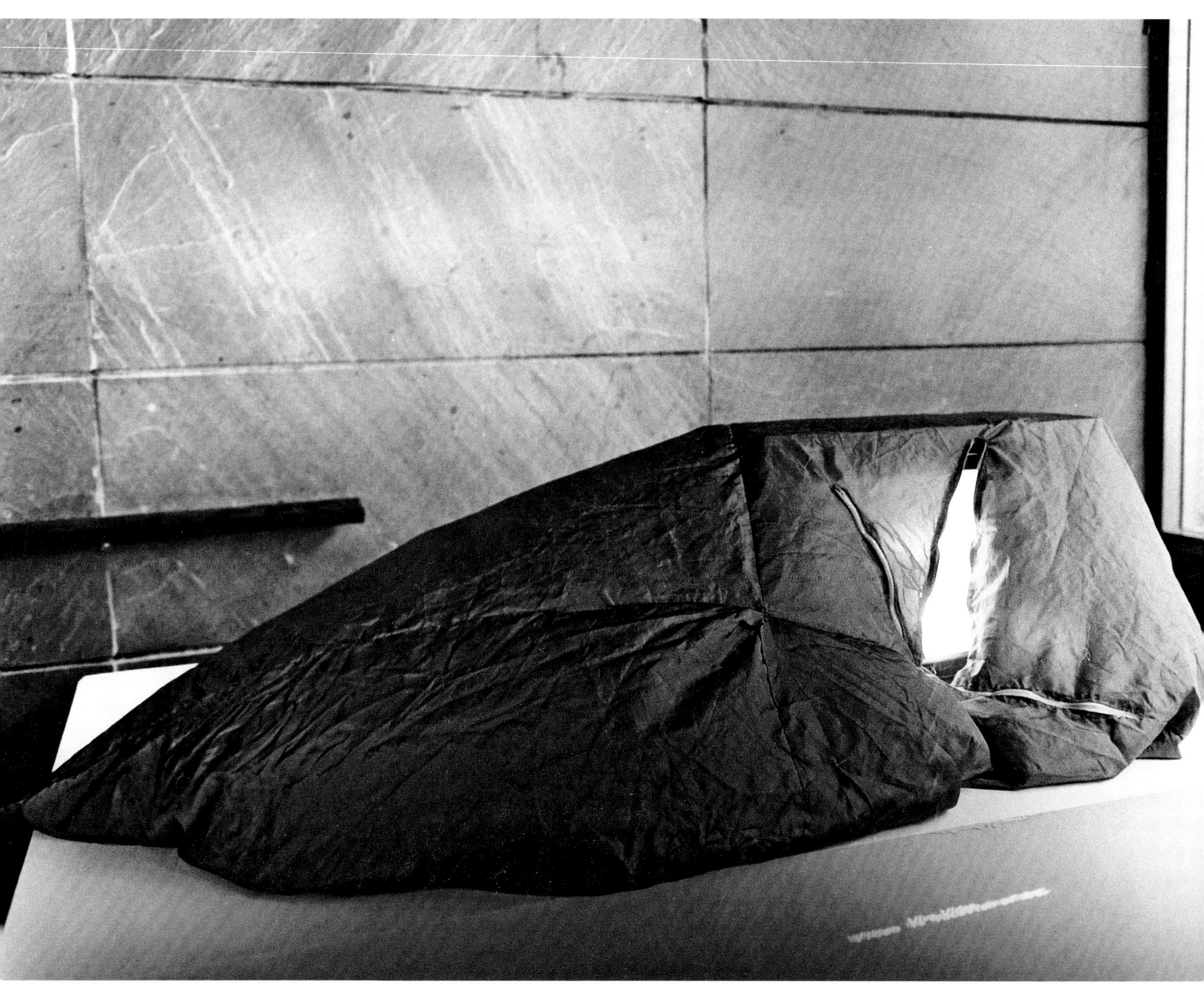

Peter Moore. Photograph of *Video Poem* installed in *4 Video Sculptures,* Japan House, New York, January 21–February 3, 1978, with a line from the text "Video Poem" seen projected on the pedestal (the complete text is on page 41)

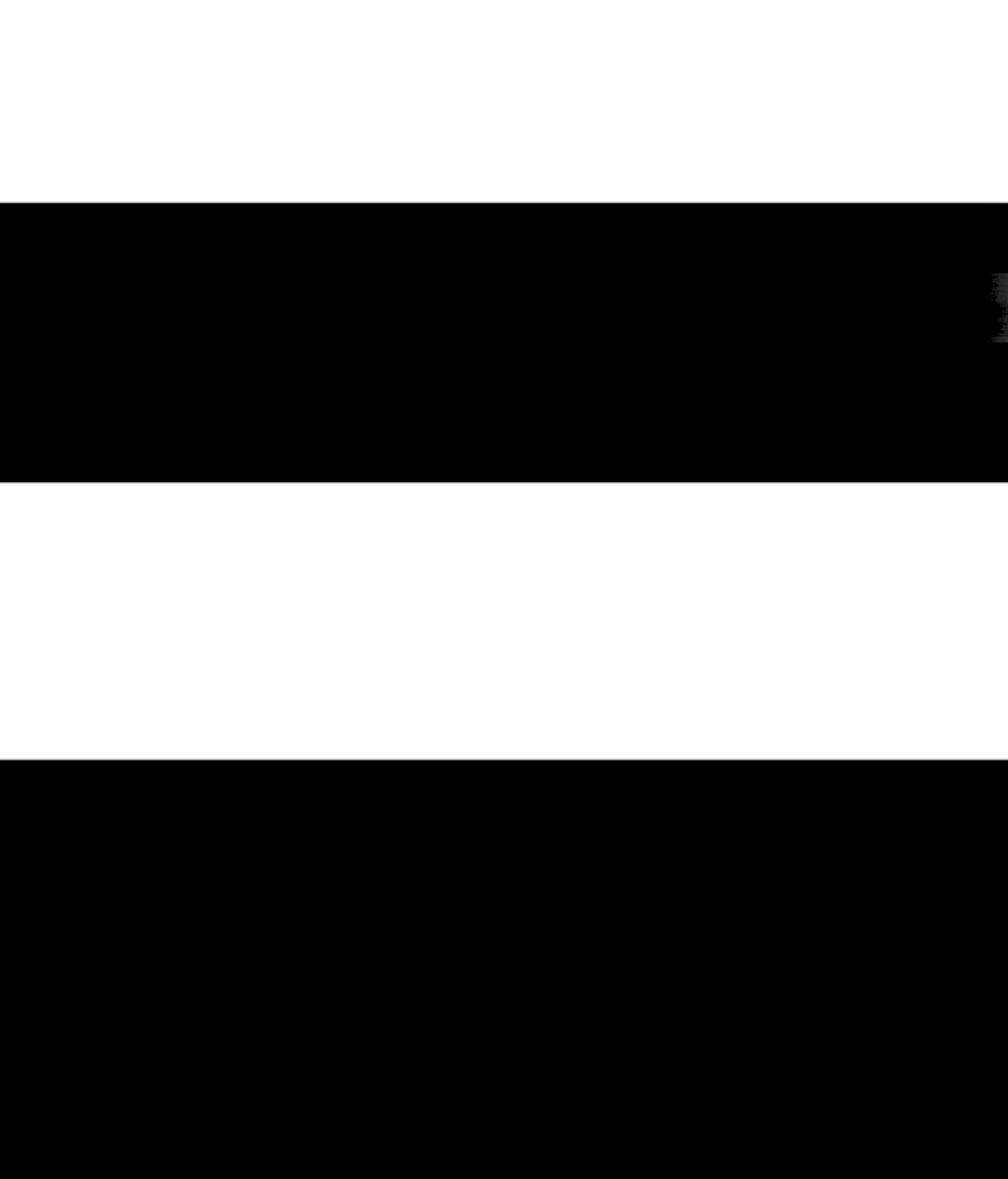

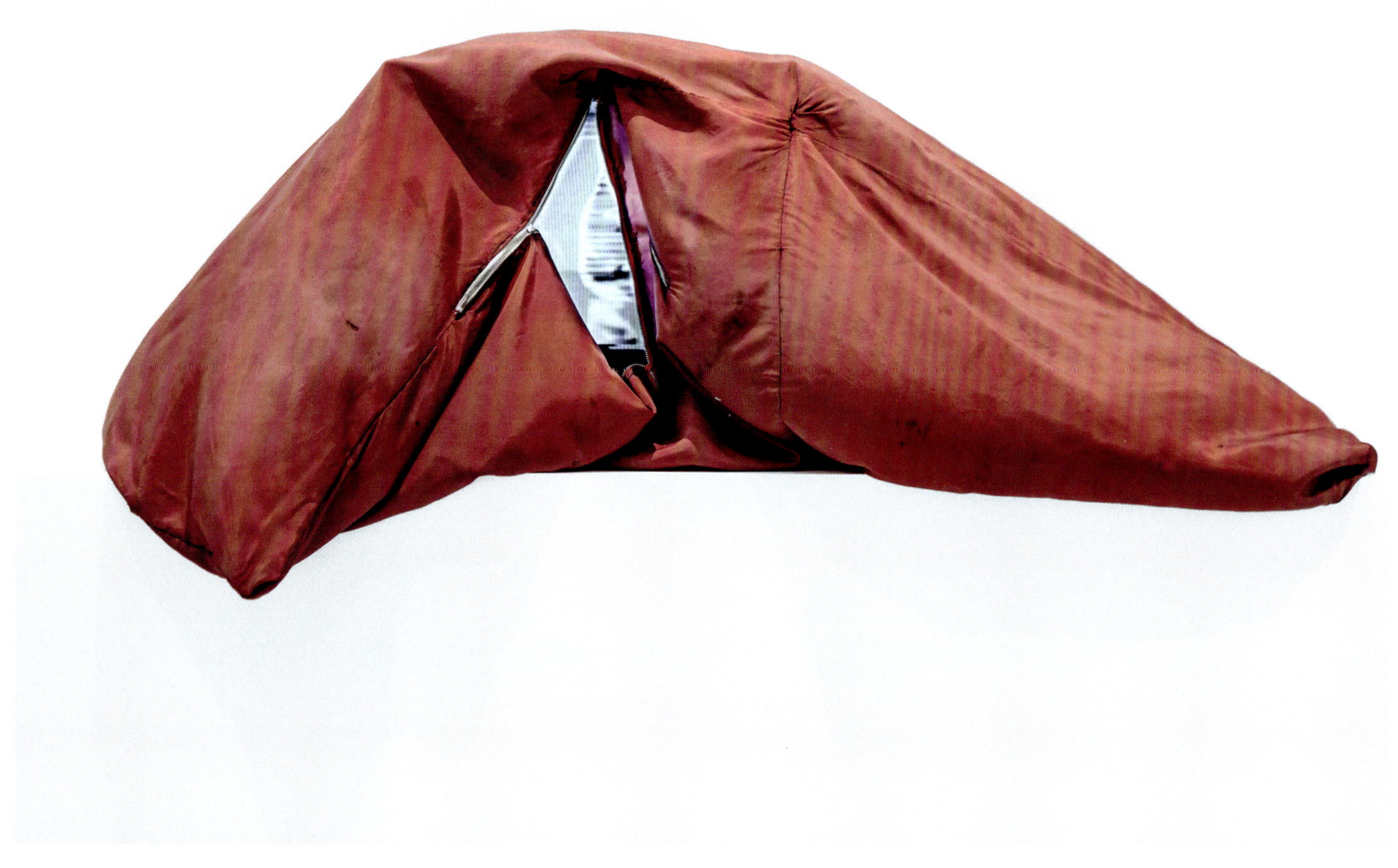

Video Poem installed in *The Body Electric*, Walker Art Center, Minneapolis, March 30–July 21, 2019

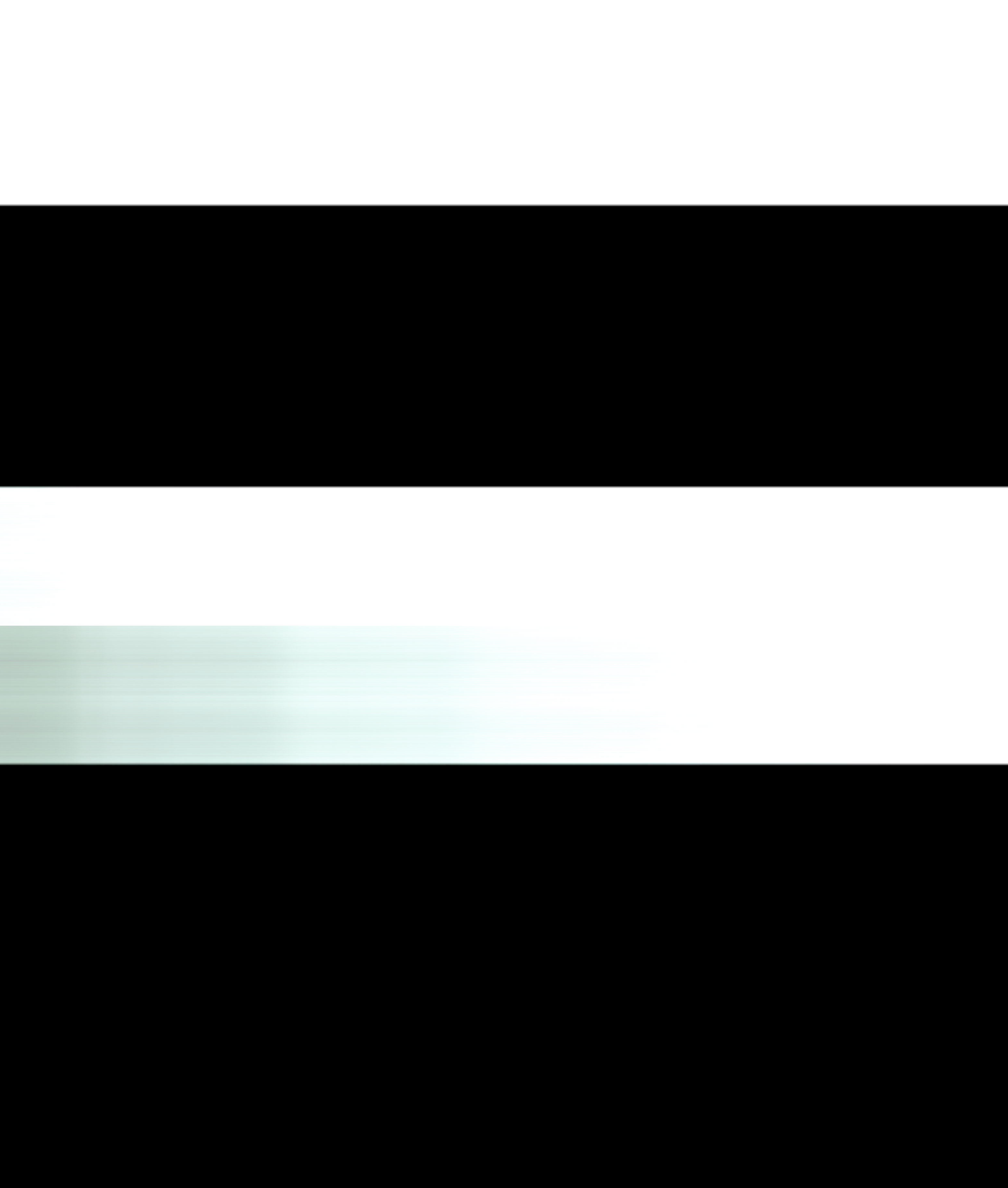

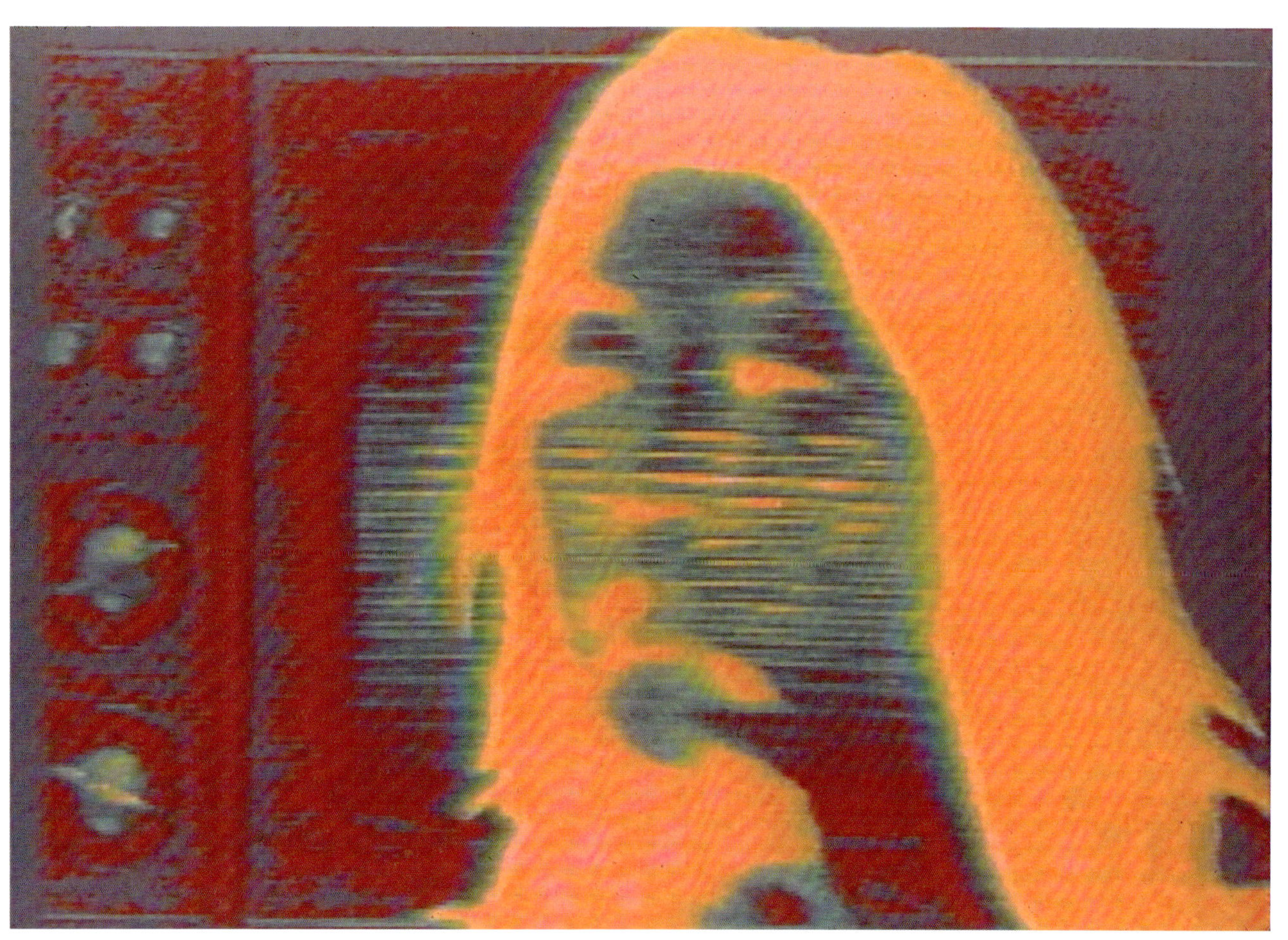

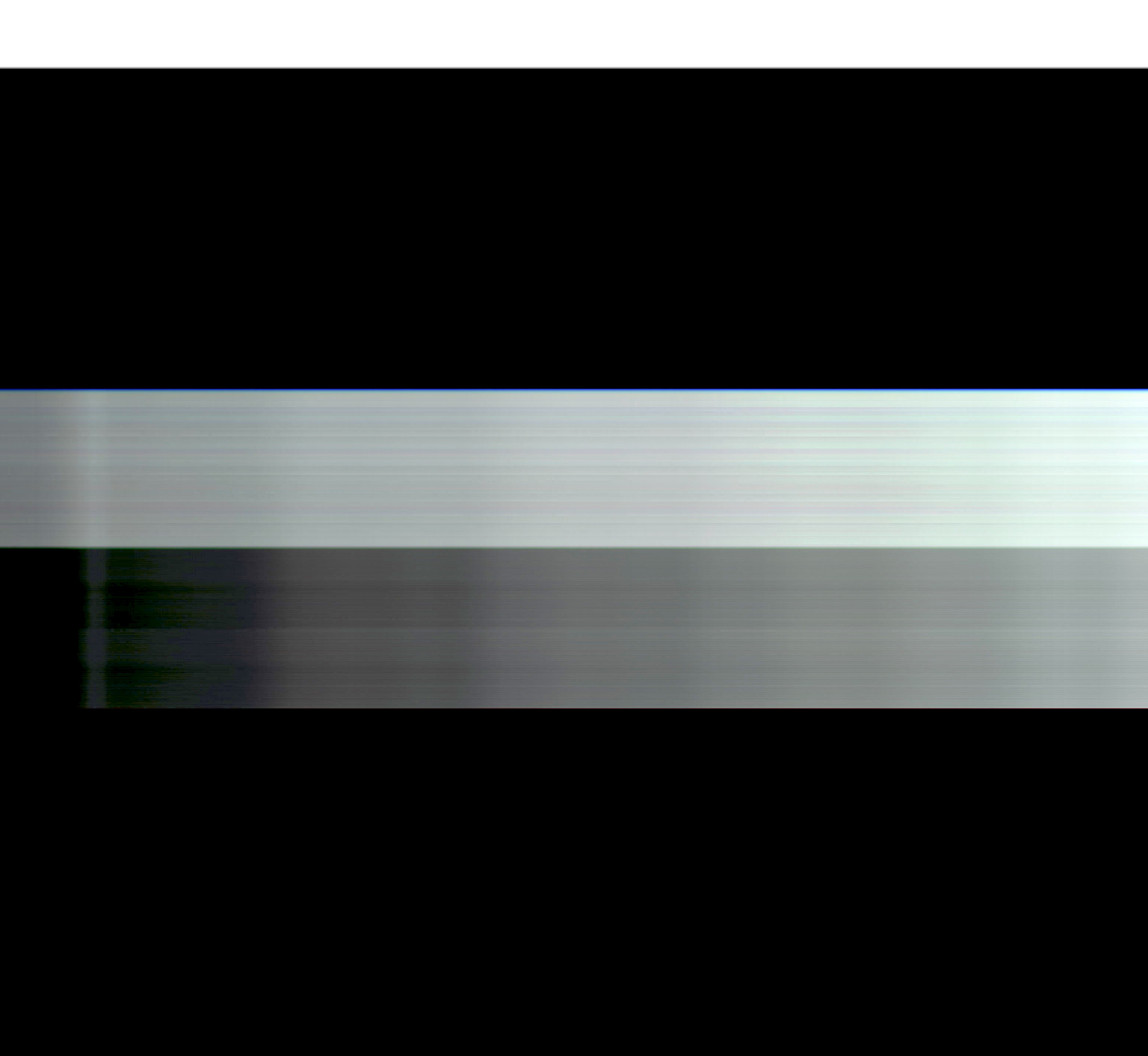

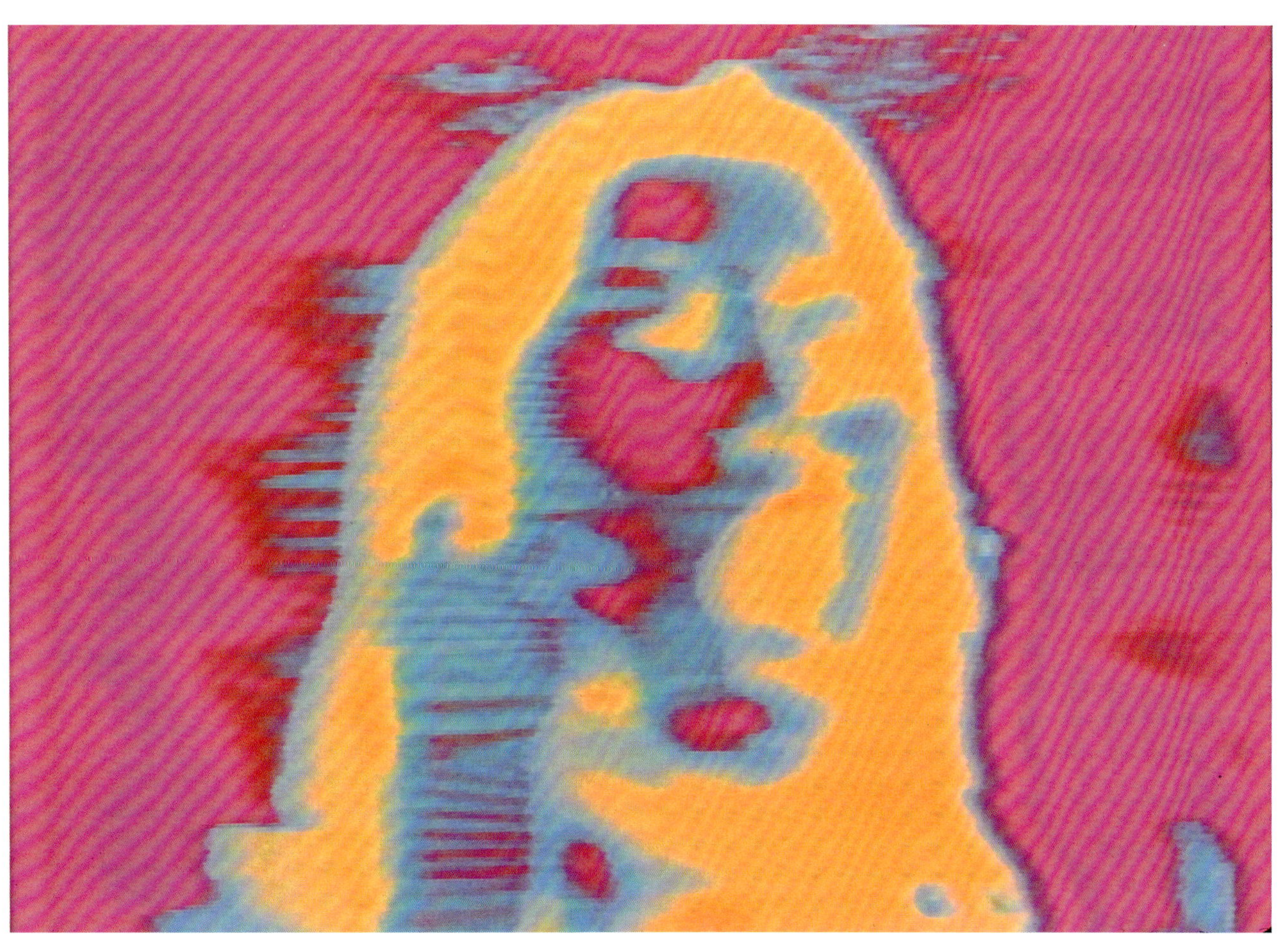

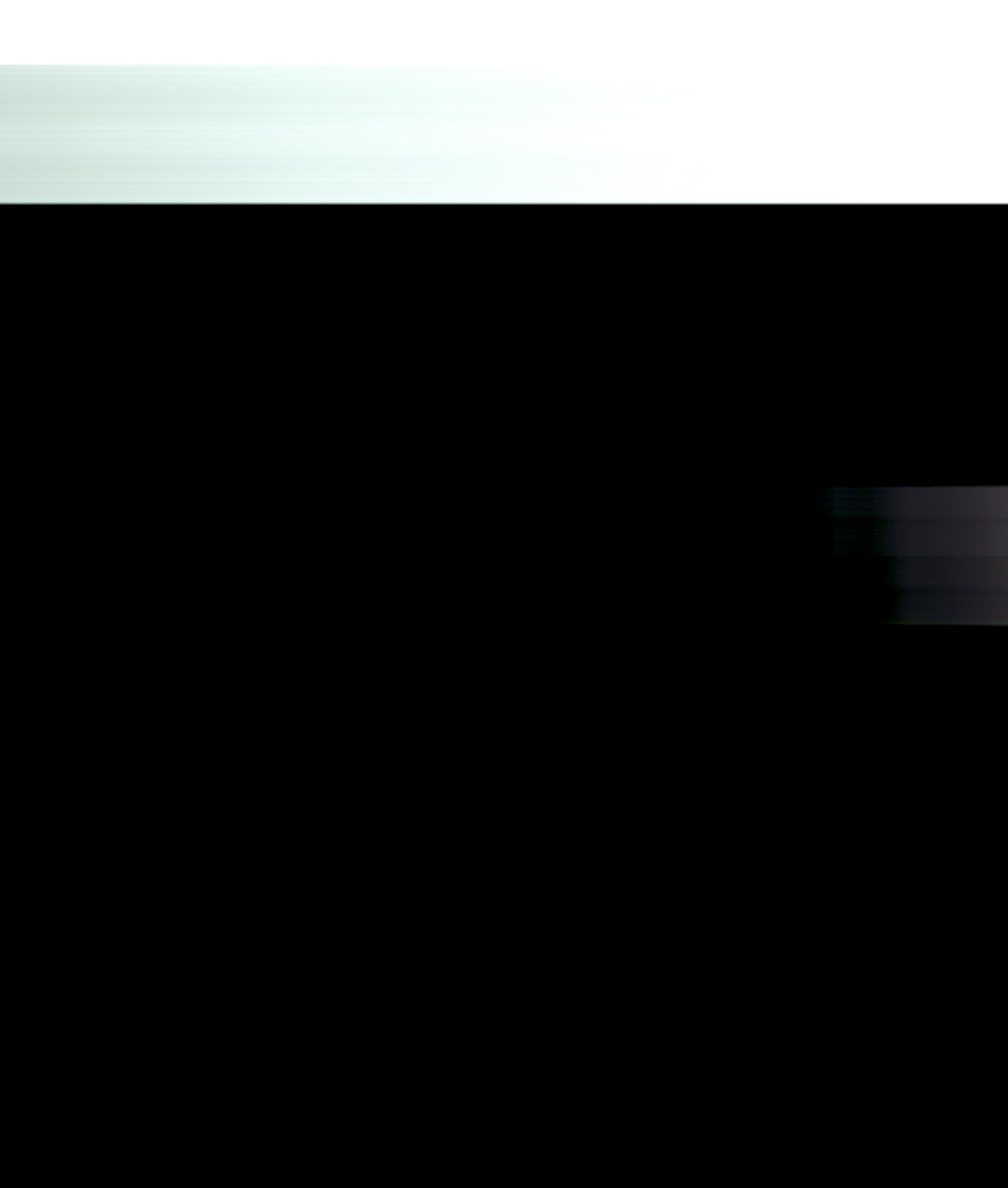

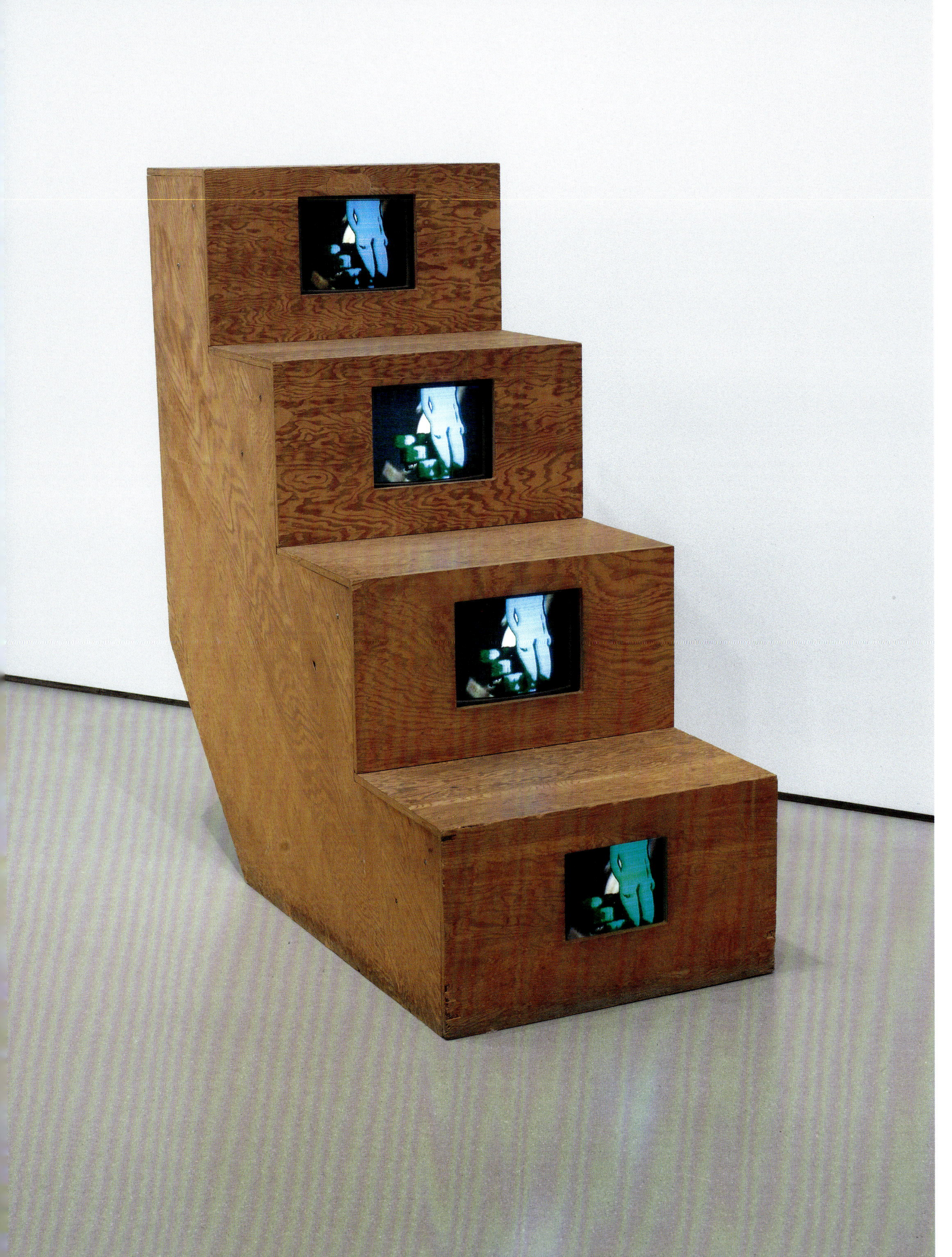

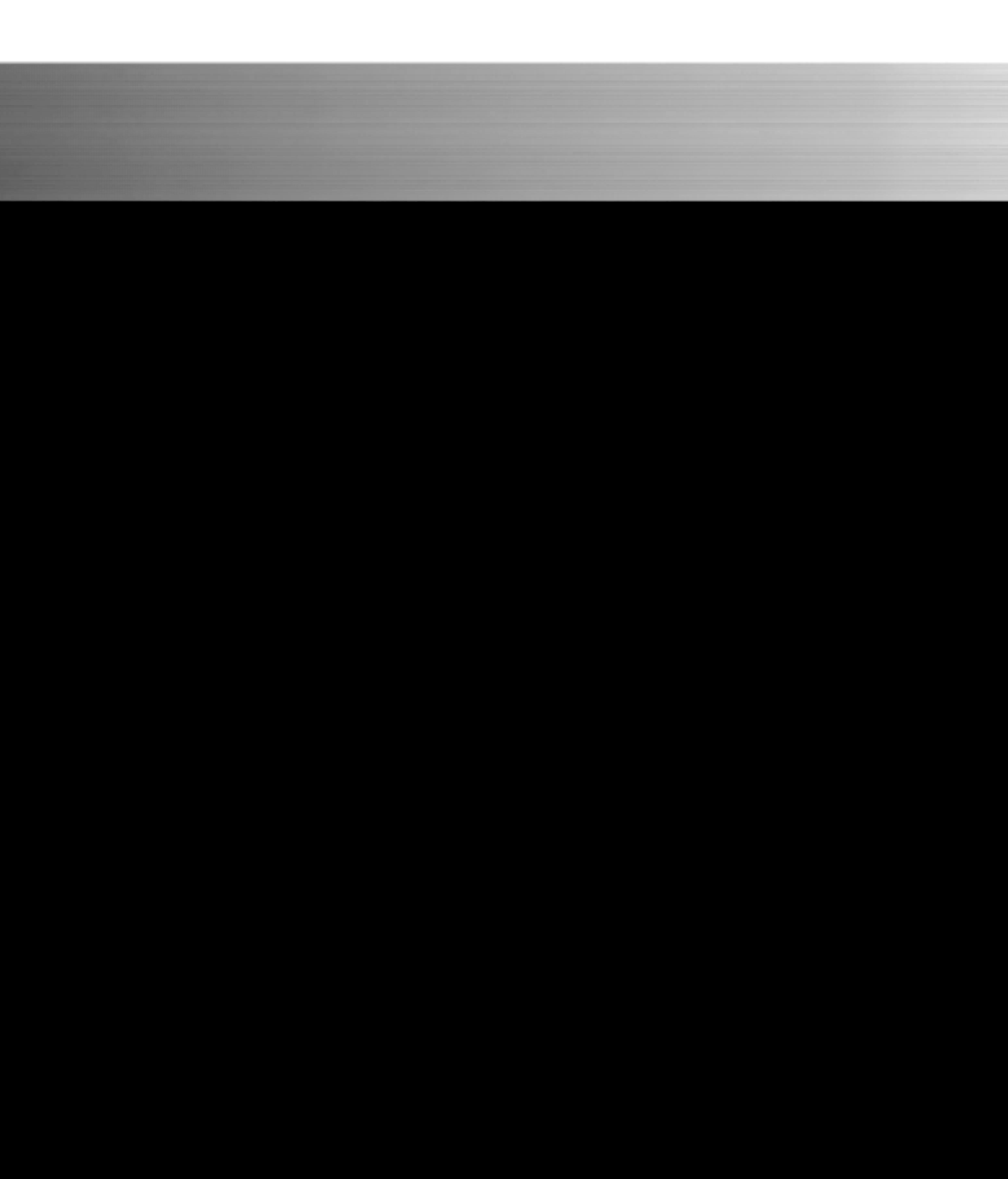

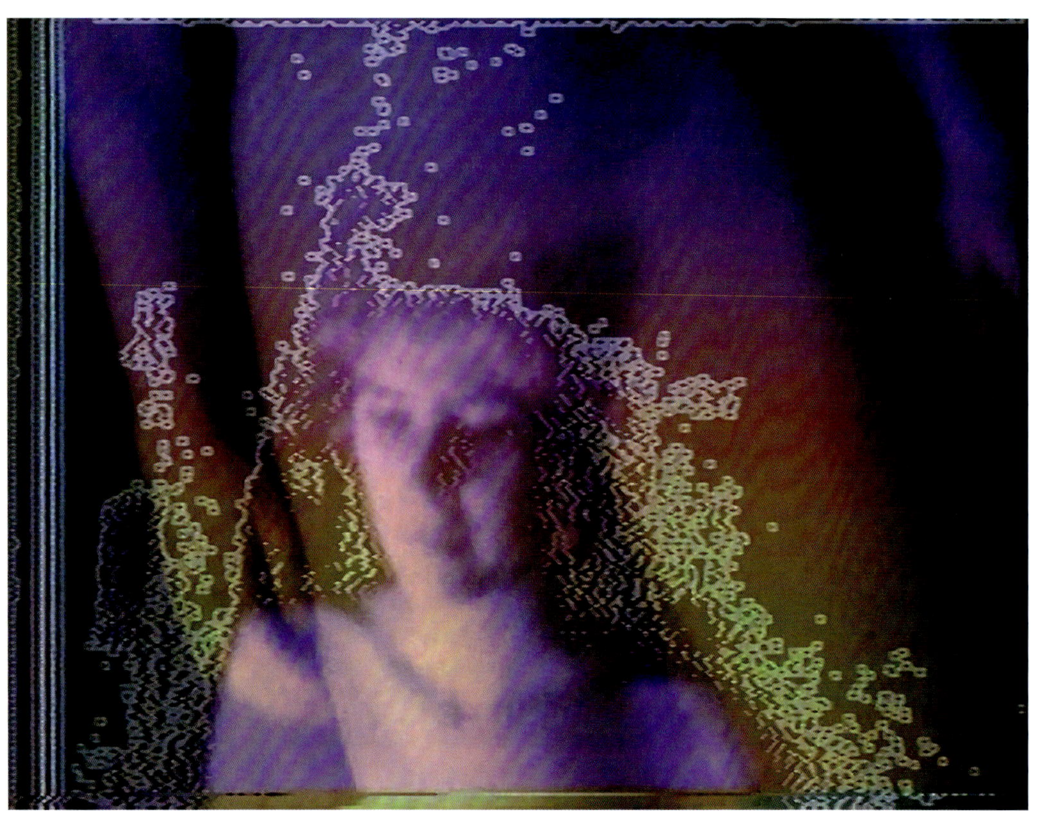

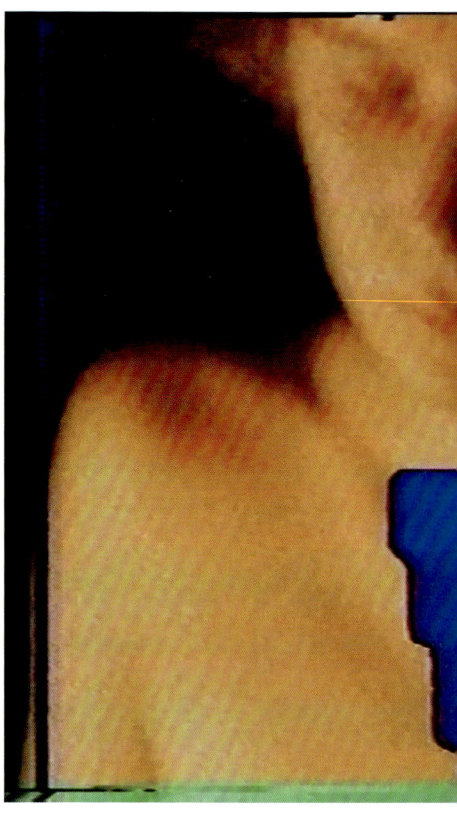

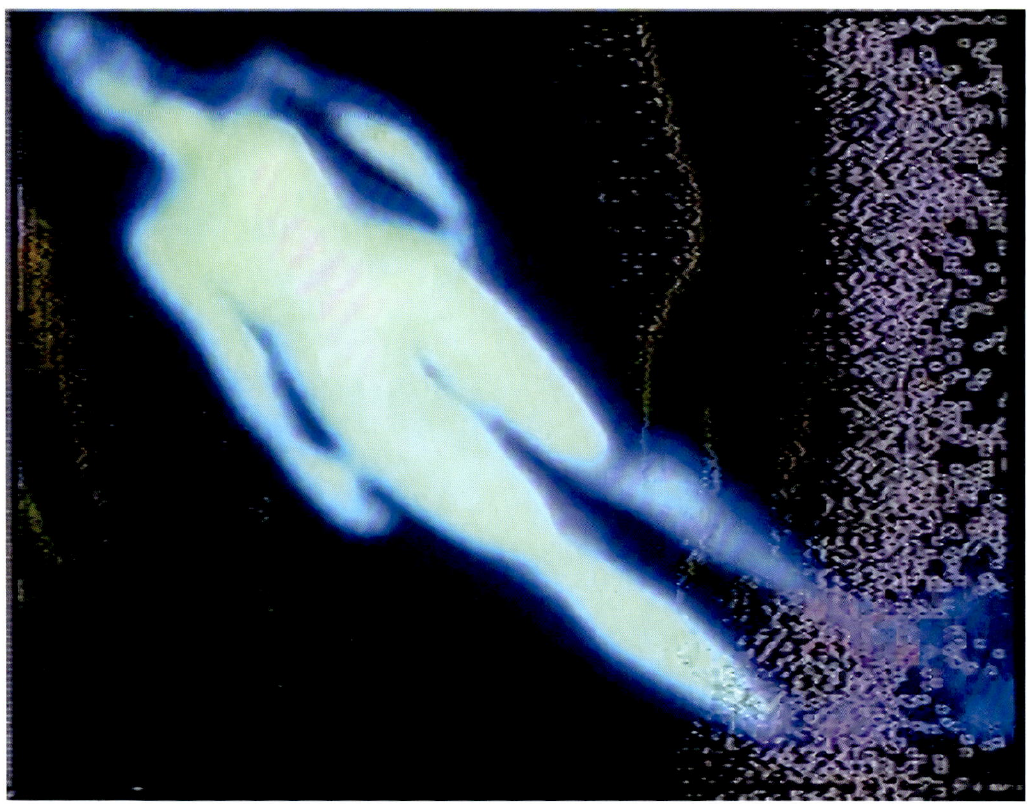

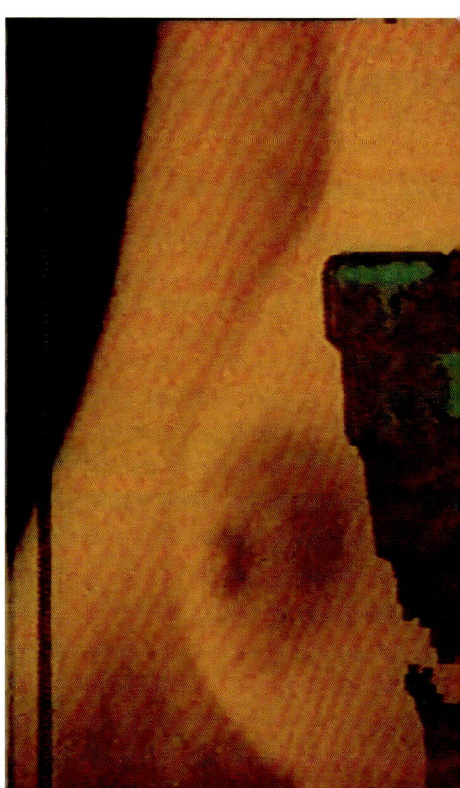

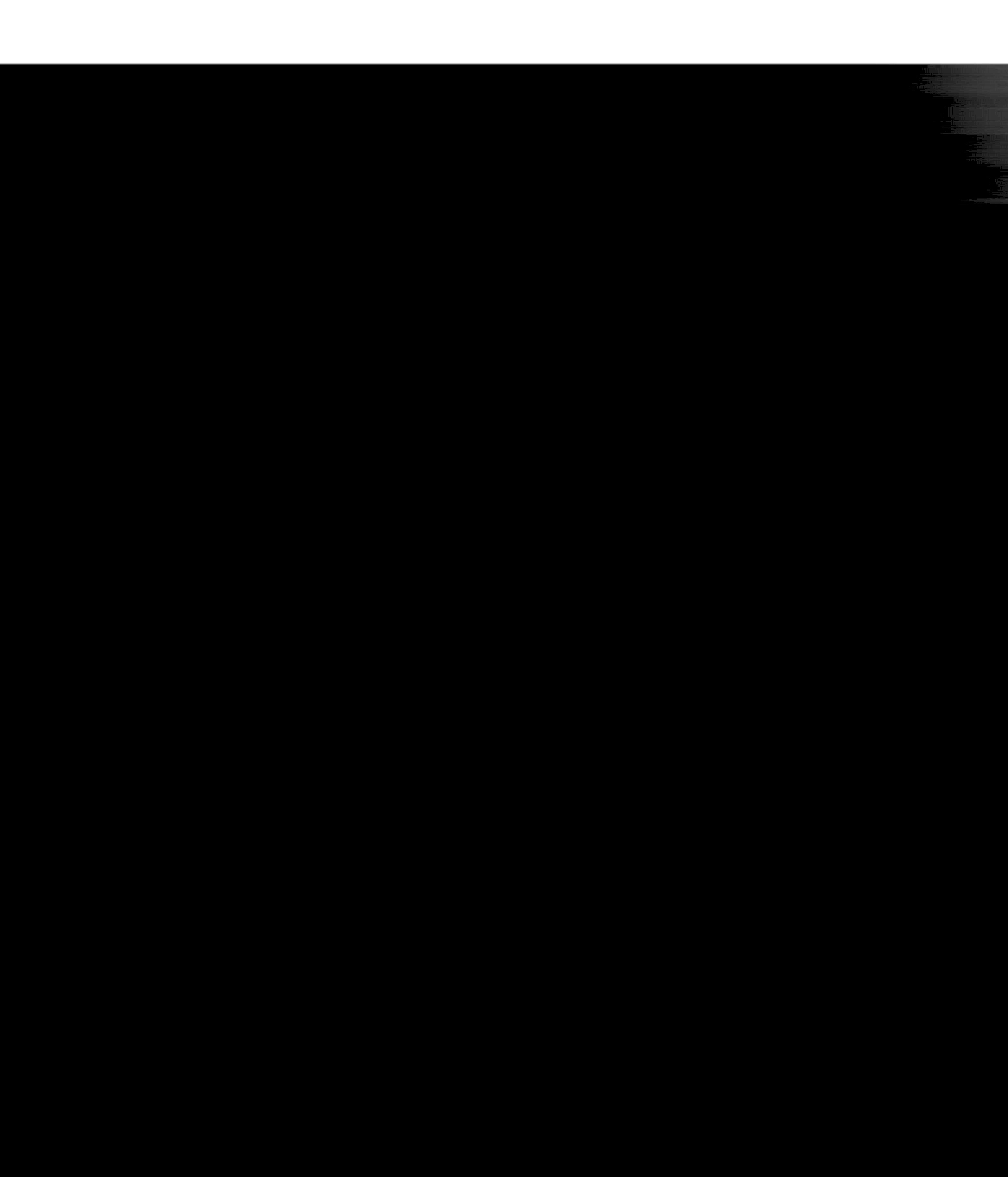

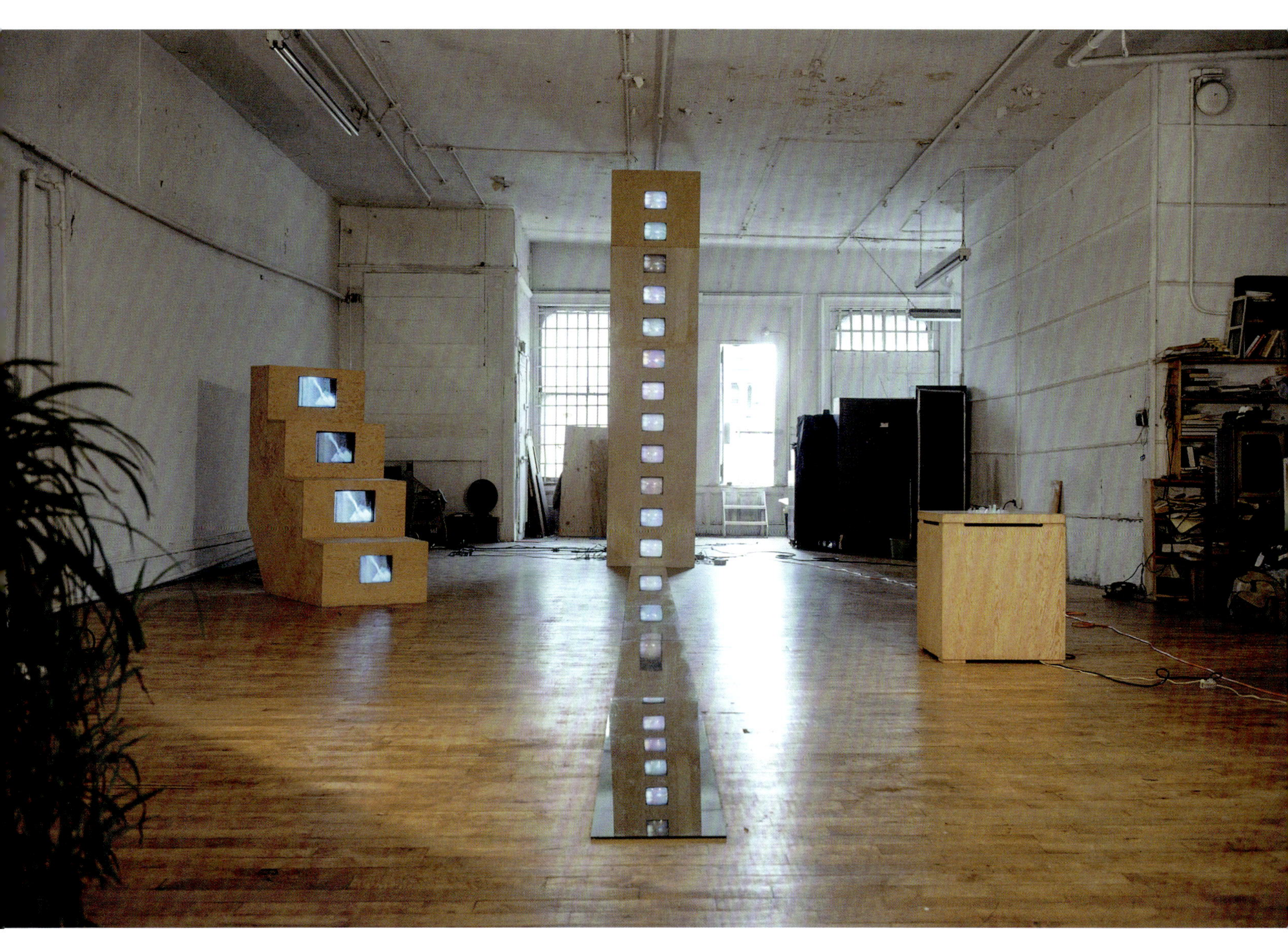

Peter Moore. Photograph of three works from the Duchampiana series installed in Kubota's loft on Mercer Street, New York, 1976. Left to right: *Nude Descending a Staircase, Marcel Duchamp's Grave* (1972–75), and *Video Chess* (1968–75)

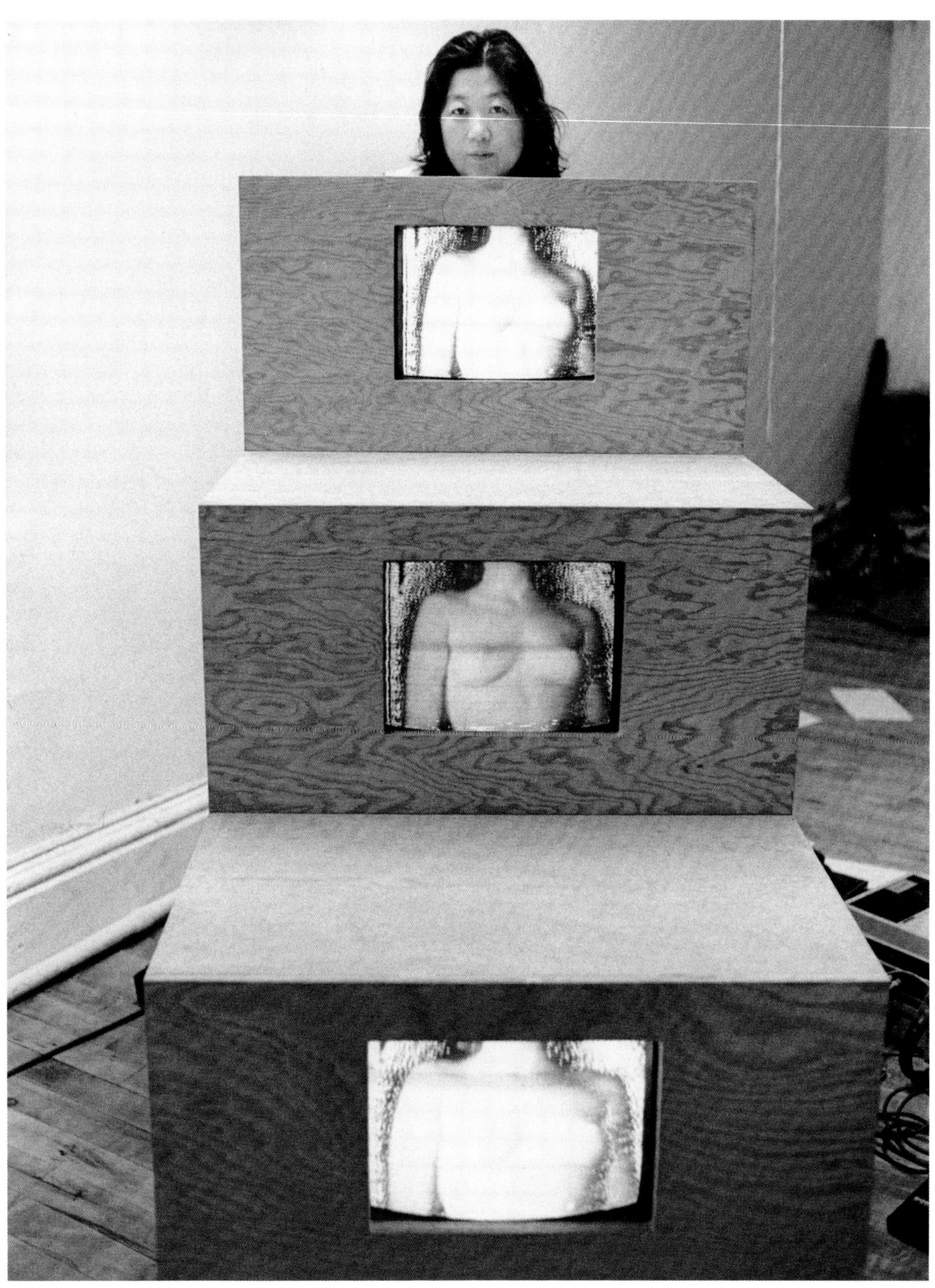

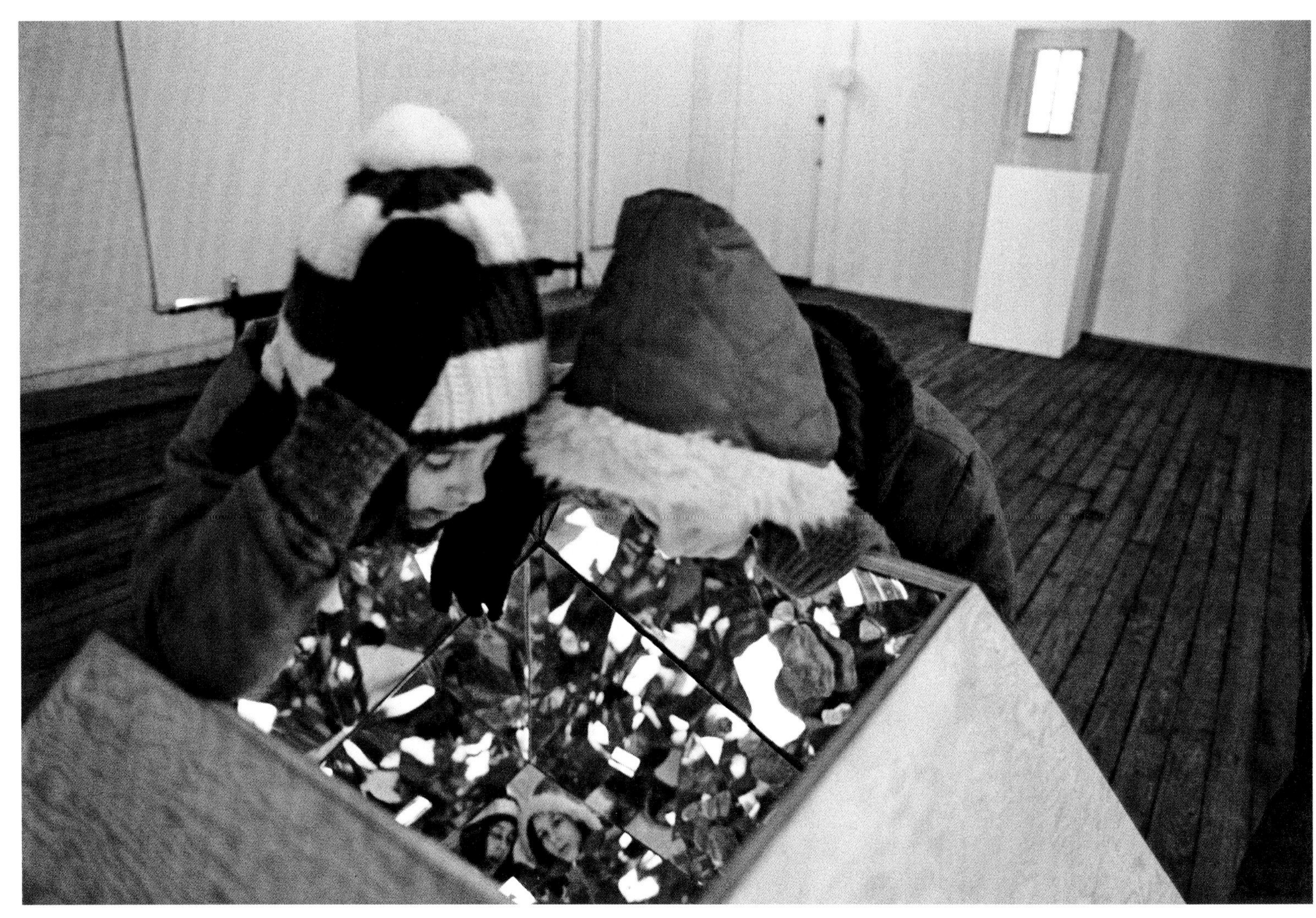

Peter Moore. Photograph of *Mountain*, the first version of *Three Mountains*, with Robin and Rebecca Moore. Installed in *Meta-Marcel*, René Block Gallery, New York, January 22–March 5, 1977, with *Meta-Marcel: Window (Snow)* (1976–77) in the background

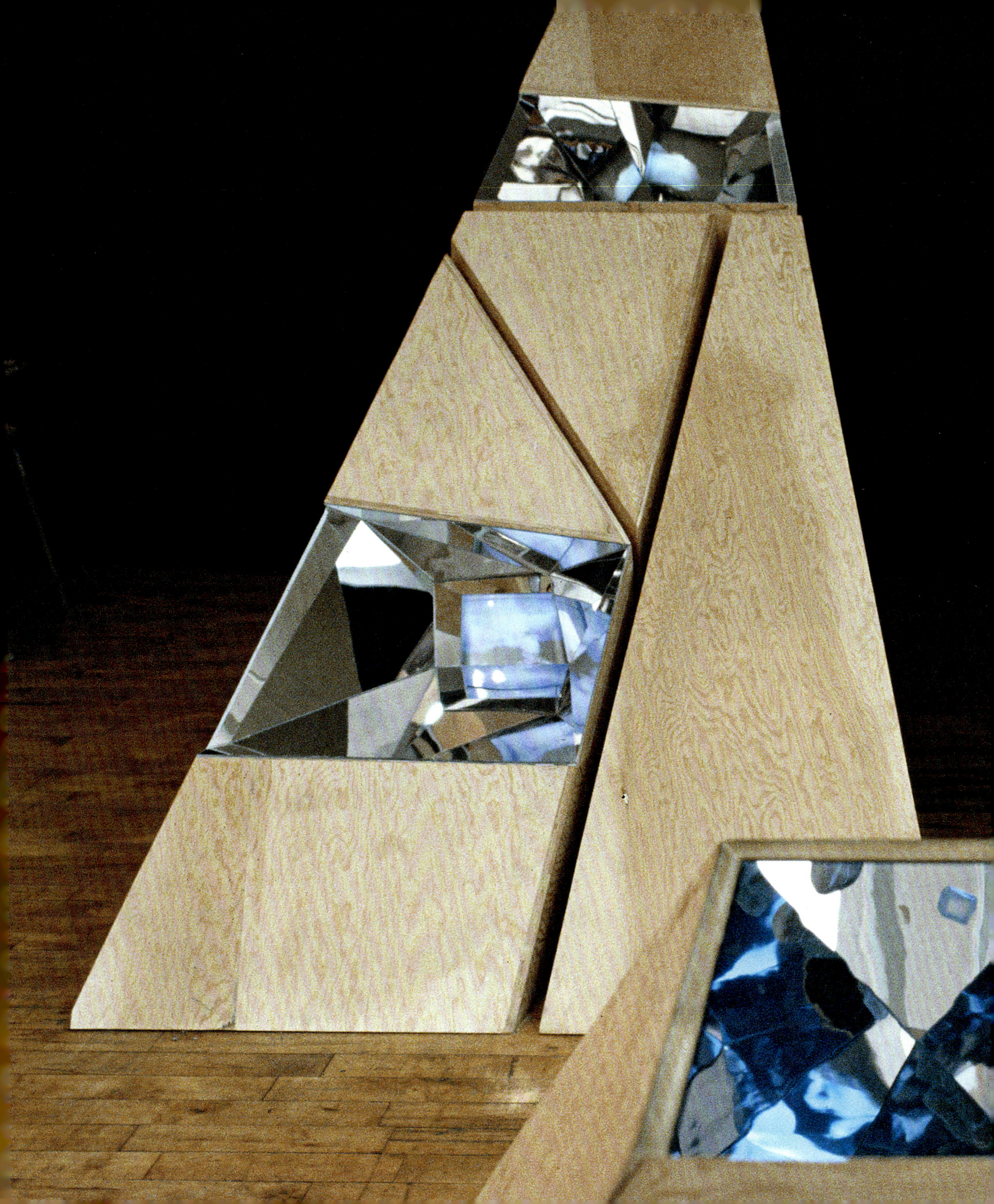

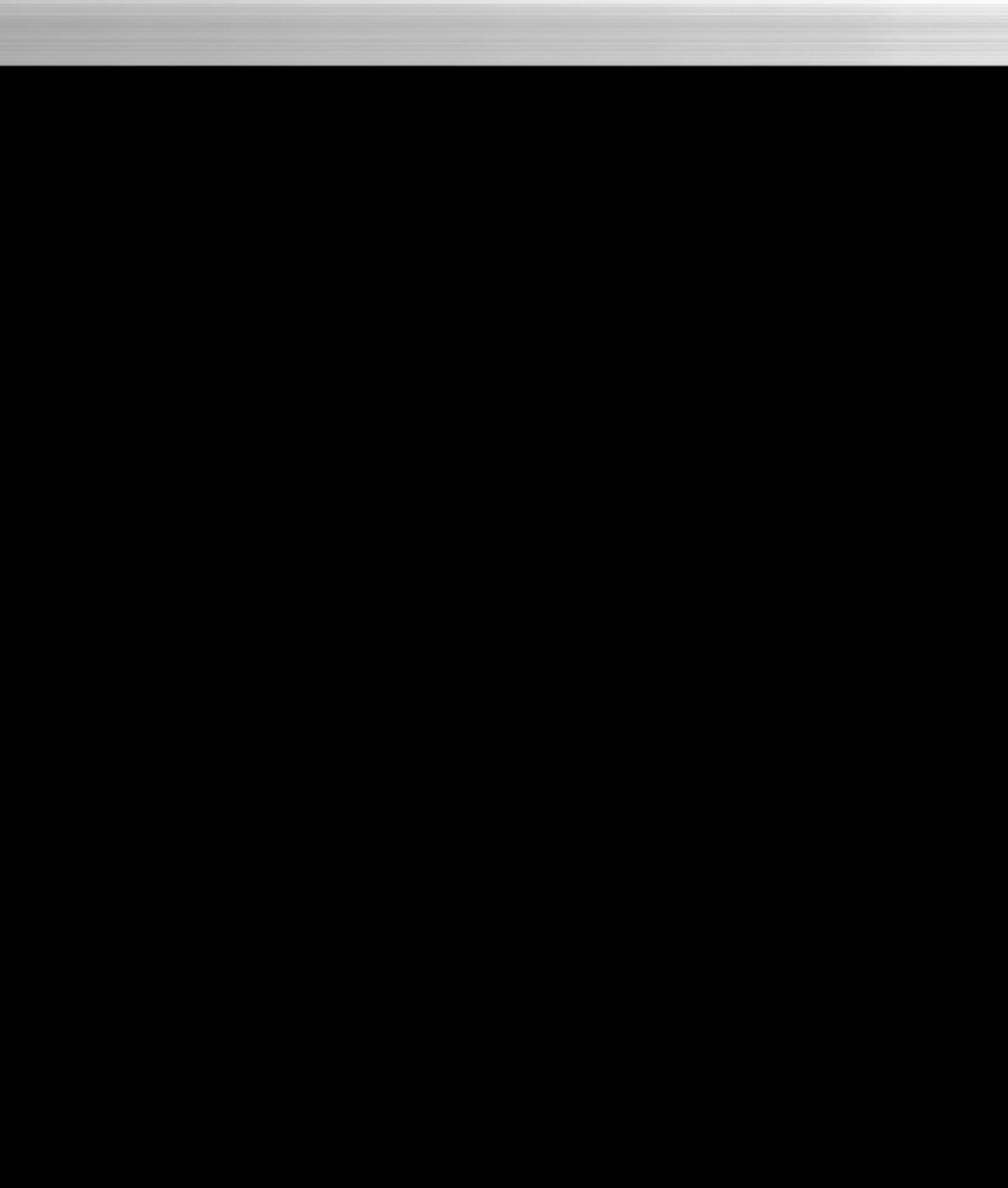

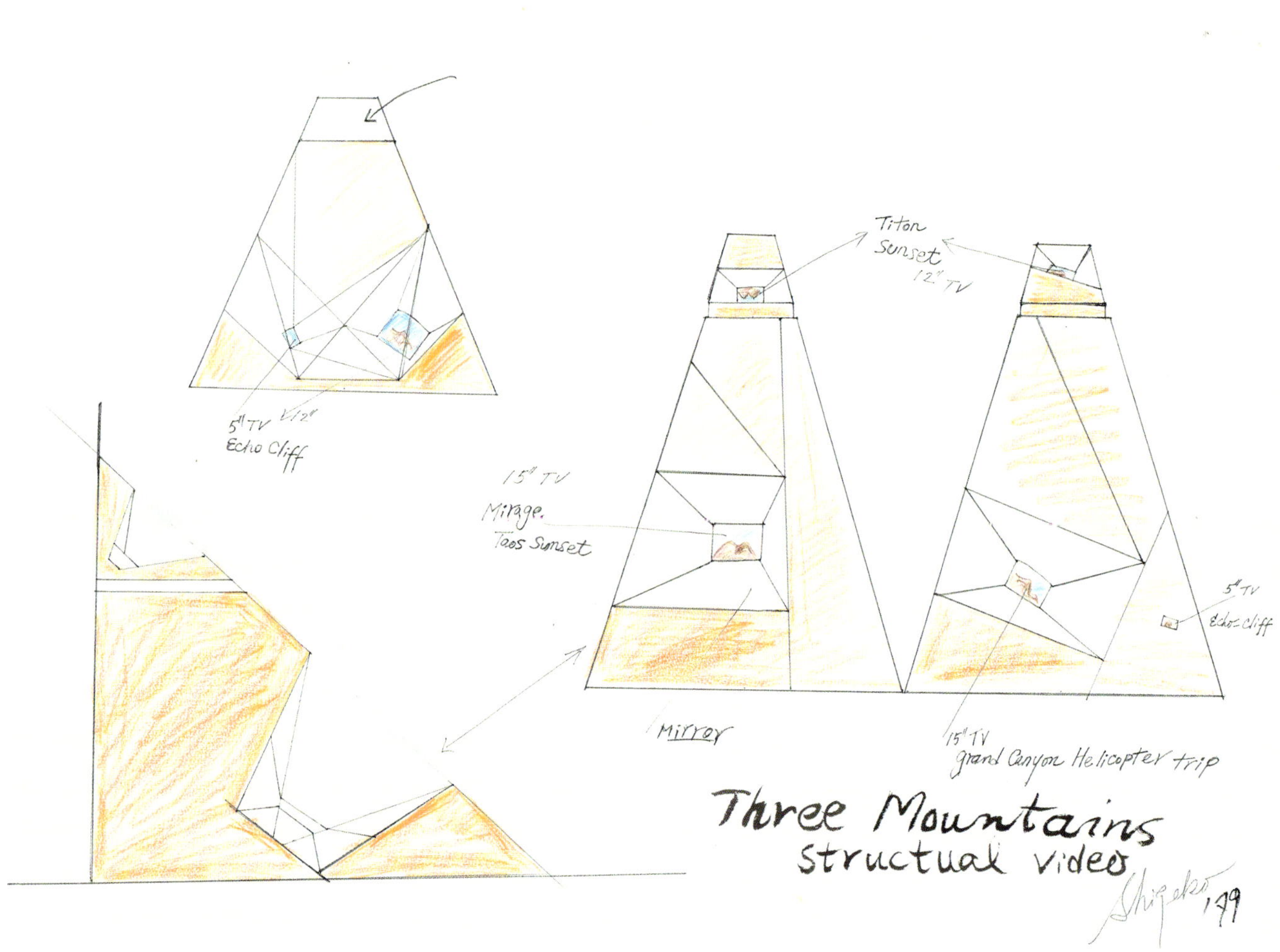

Schematic drawing for *Three Mountains*. 1979. Watercolor stick and sumi ink on paper, 12 ¼ × 18 in. (31.1 × 45.7 cm). Shigeko Kubota Video Art Foundation

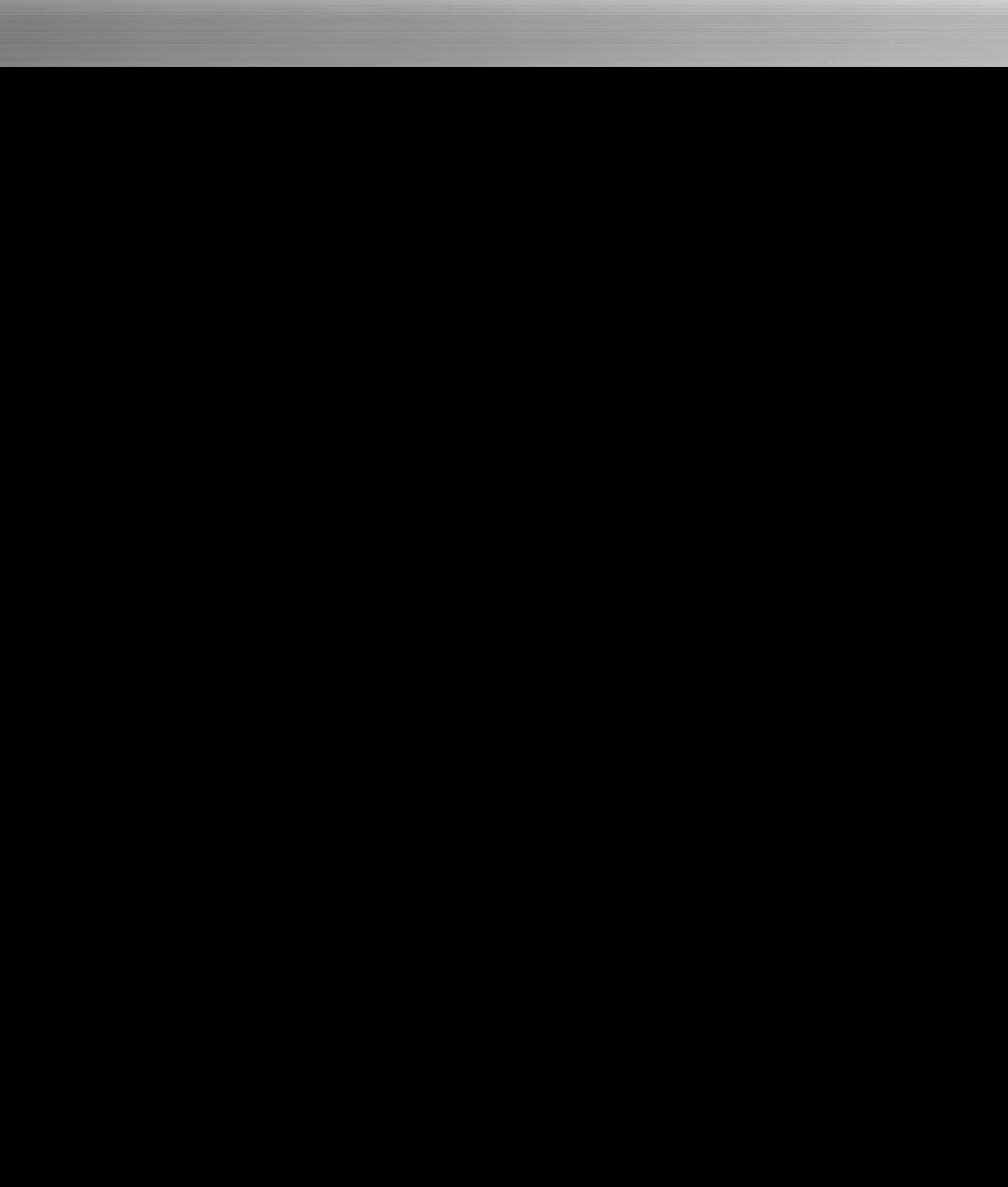

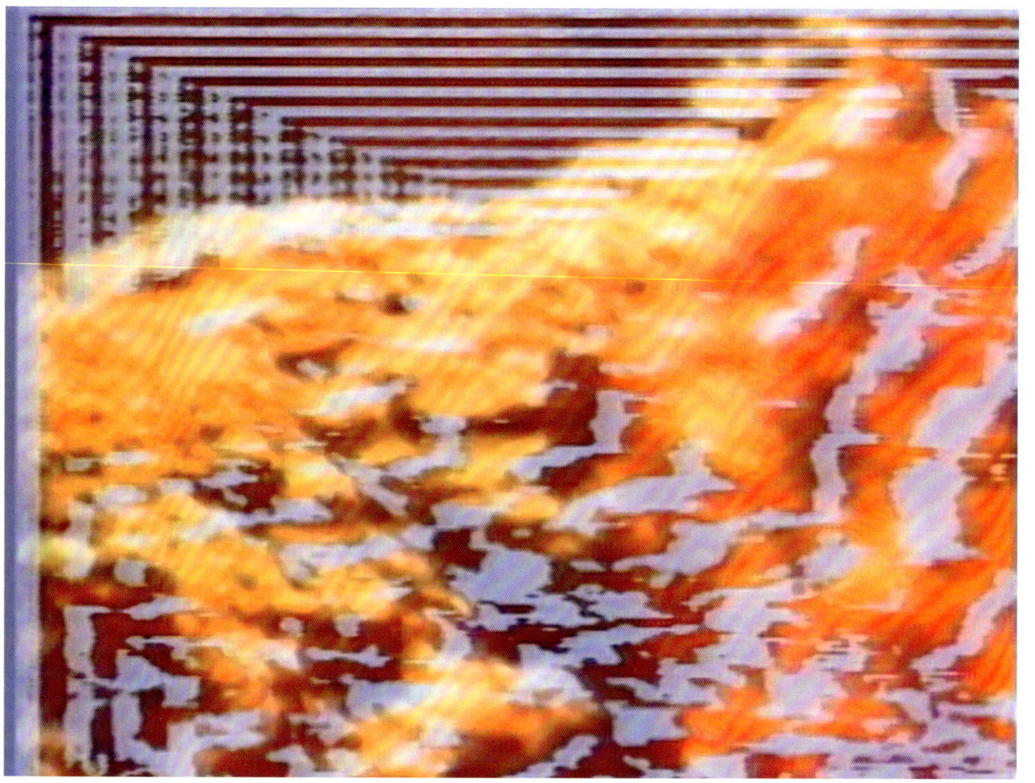

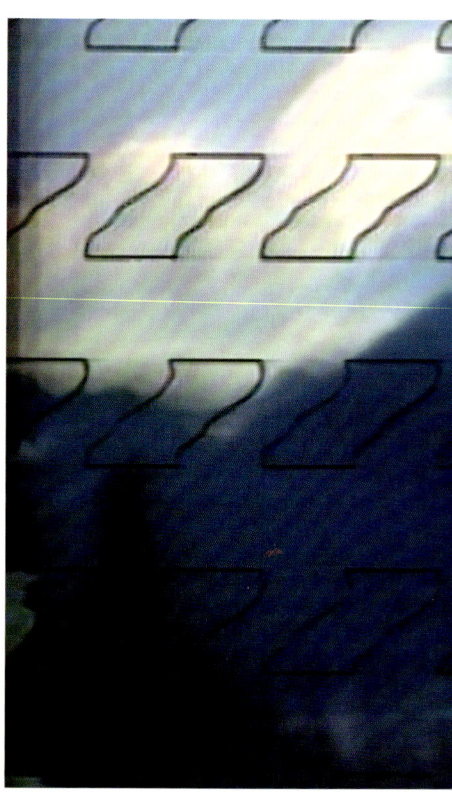

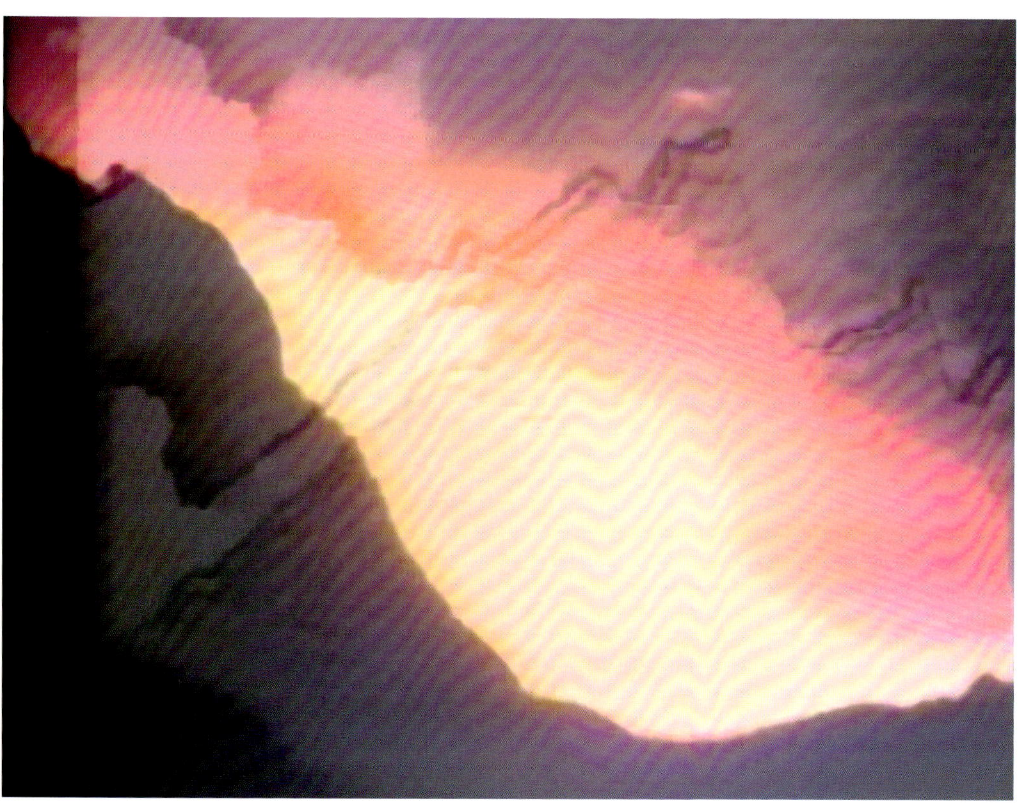

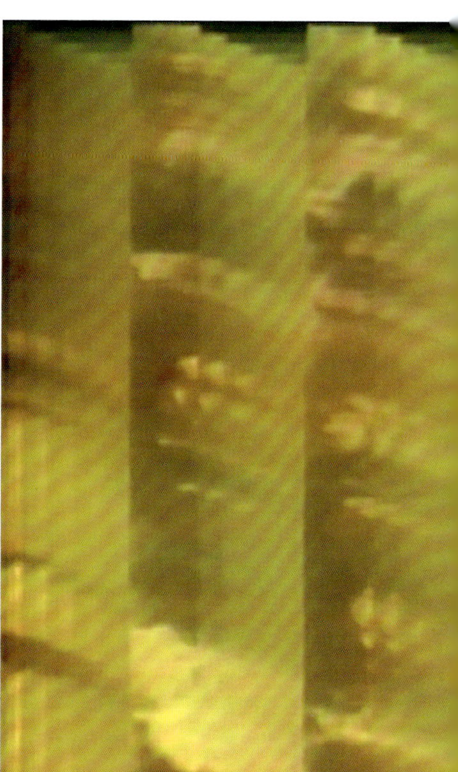

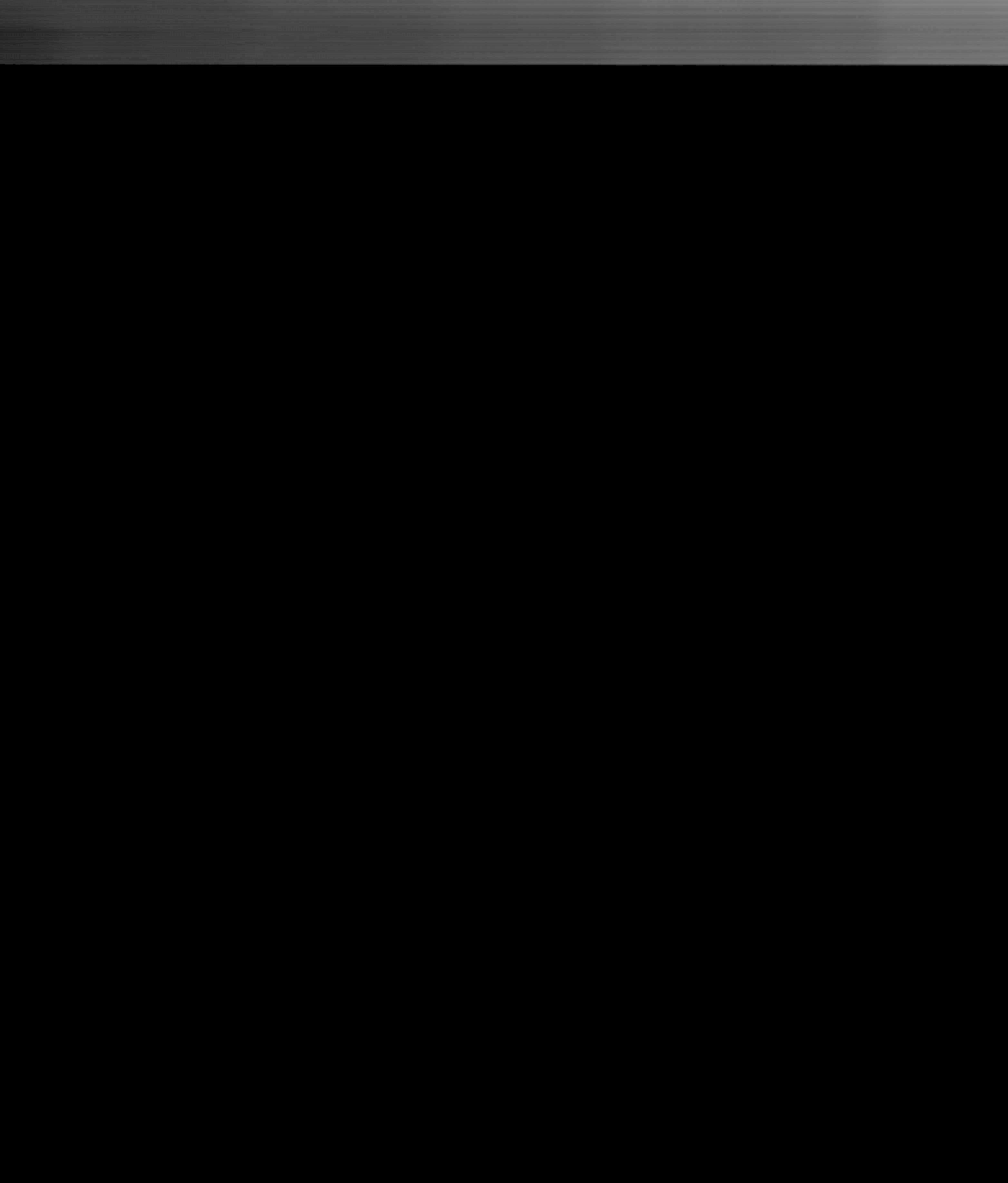

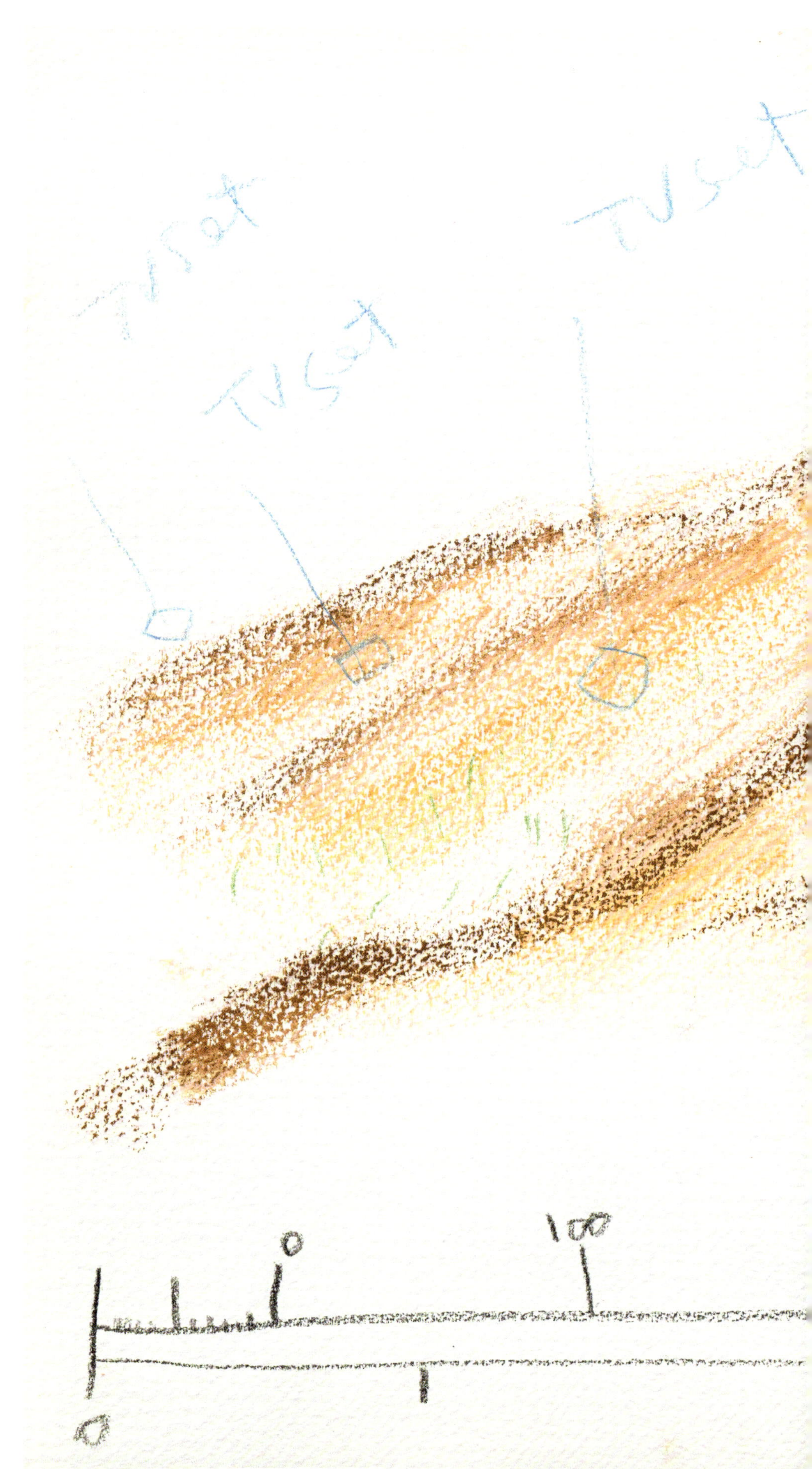

Untitled. 1977. Colored pencil, oil pastel, and watercolor stick on paper, 18 × 24 in. (45.7 × 61 cm). Shigeko Kubota Video Art Foundation

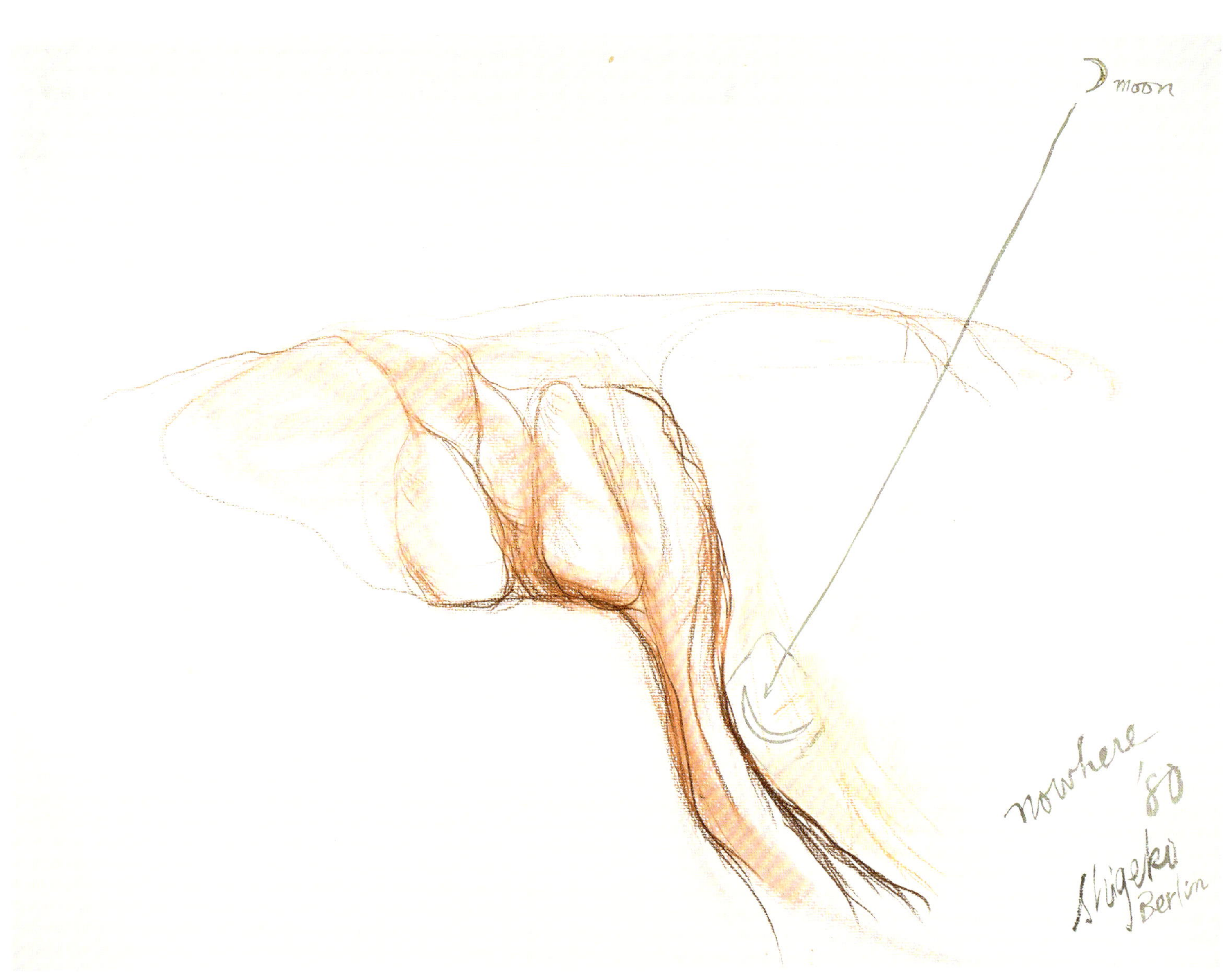

Untitled. 1980. Colored pencil, oil pastel, watercolor stick, and sumi ink on paper, 22 × 29 ½ in. (55.9 × 74.9 cm). Shigeko Kubota Video Art Foundation

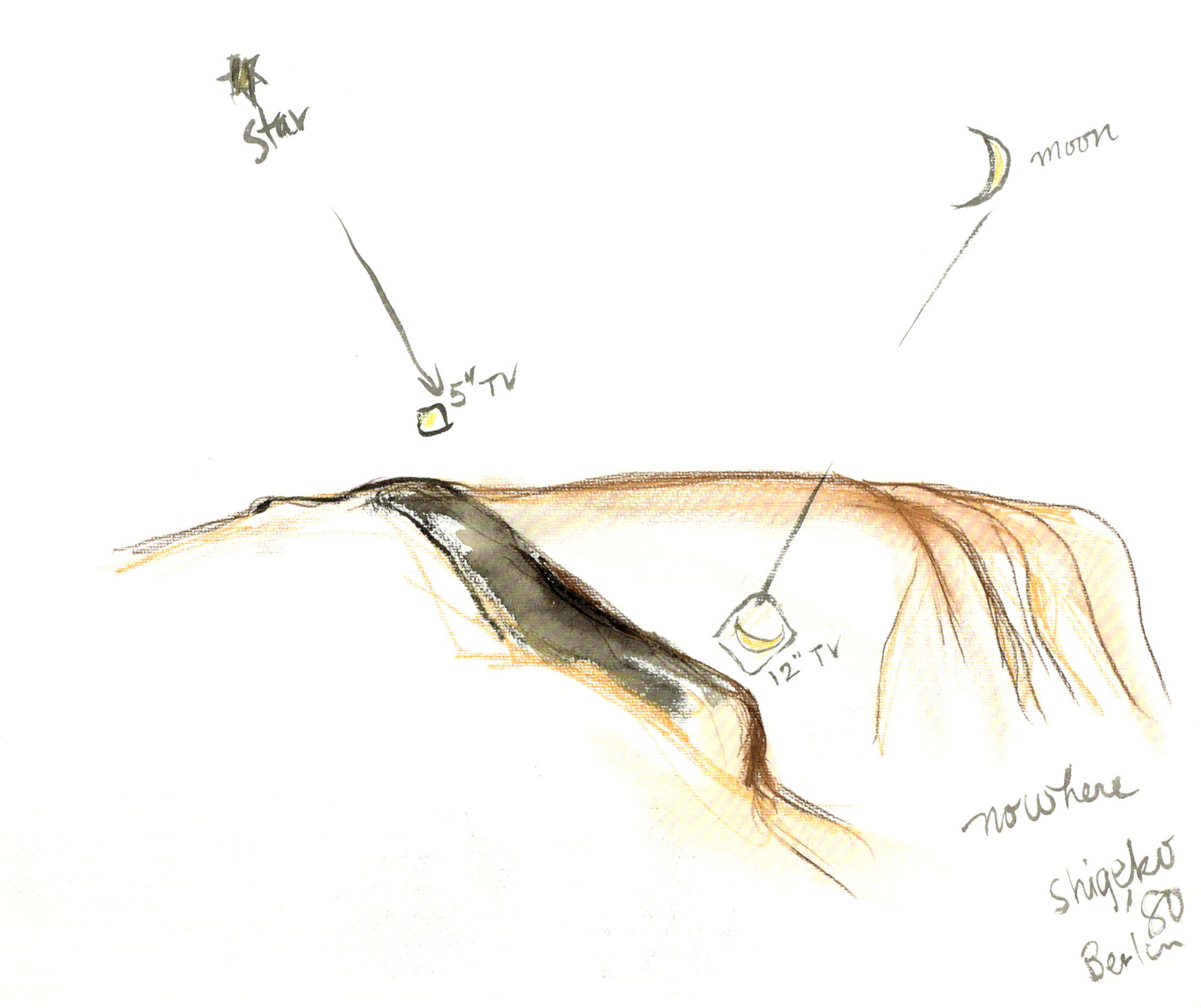

Untitled. 1980. Colored pencil, oil pastel, watercolor stick, and sumi ink on paper, 21 13⁄16 × 29 5⁄16 in. (55.4 × 74.4 cm). Shigeko Kubota Video Art Foundation

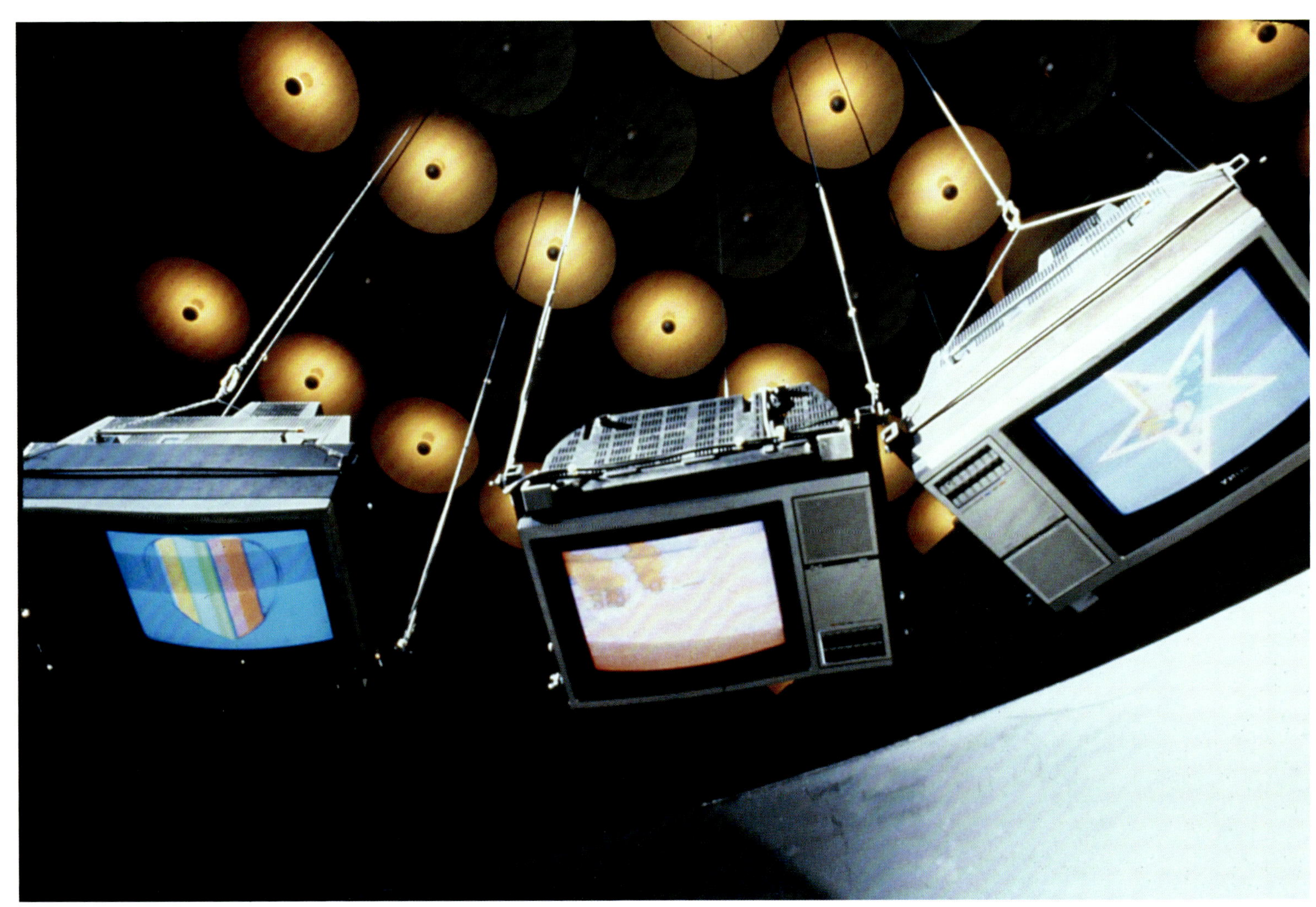

River installed in the Whitney Biennial, Whitney Museum of American Art, New York, March 15–May 29, 1983

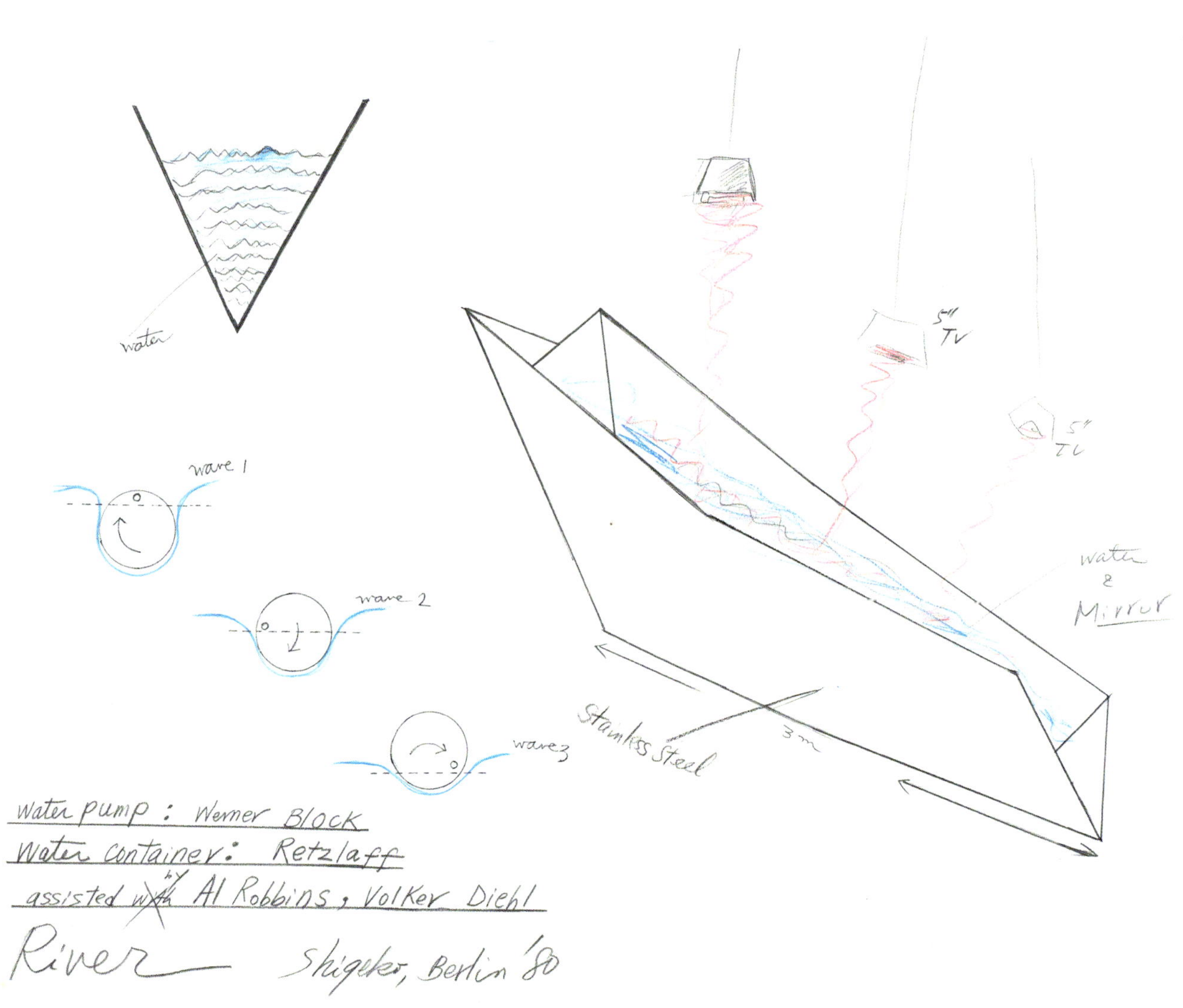

Schematic drawing for *River*. 1980. Graphite and colored pencil on paper, 21 ½ × 29 5⁄16 in. (54.6 × 74.4 cm). Shigeko Kubota Video Art Foundation

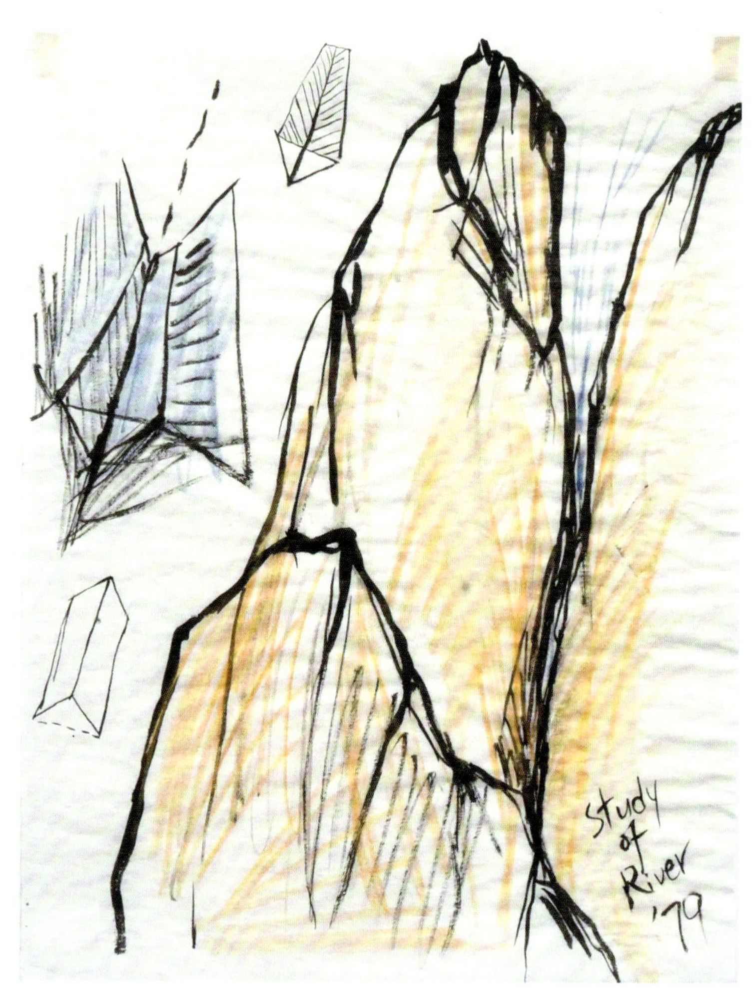
Study
of
River
'79

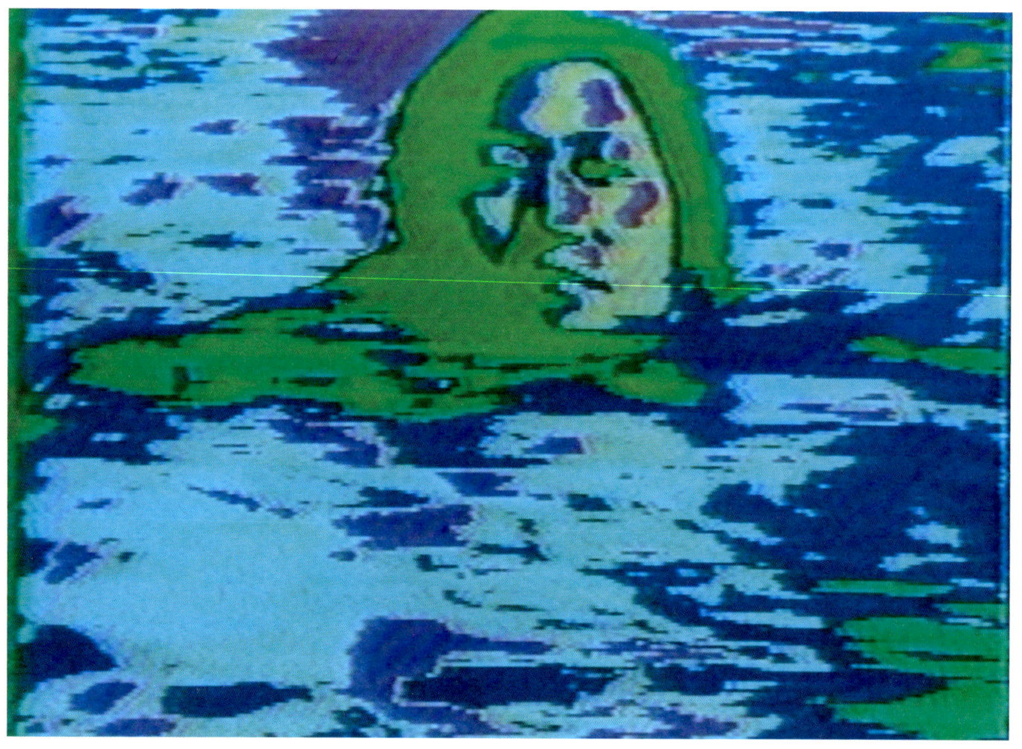
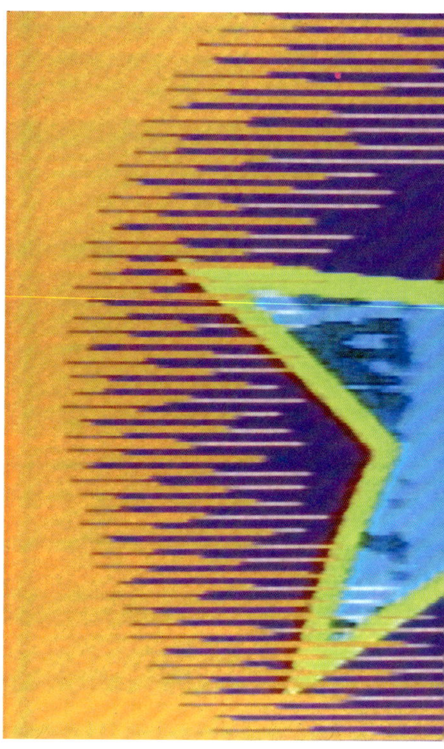
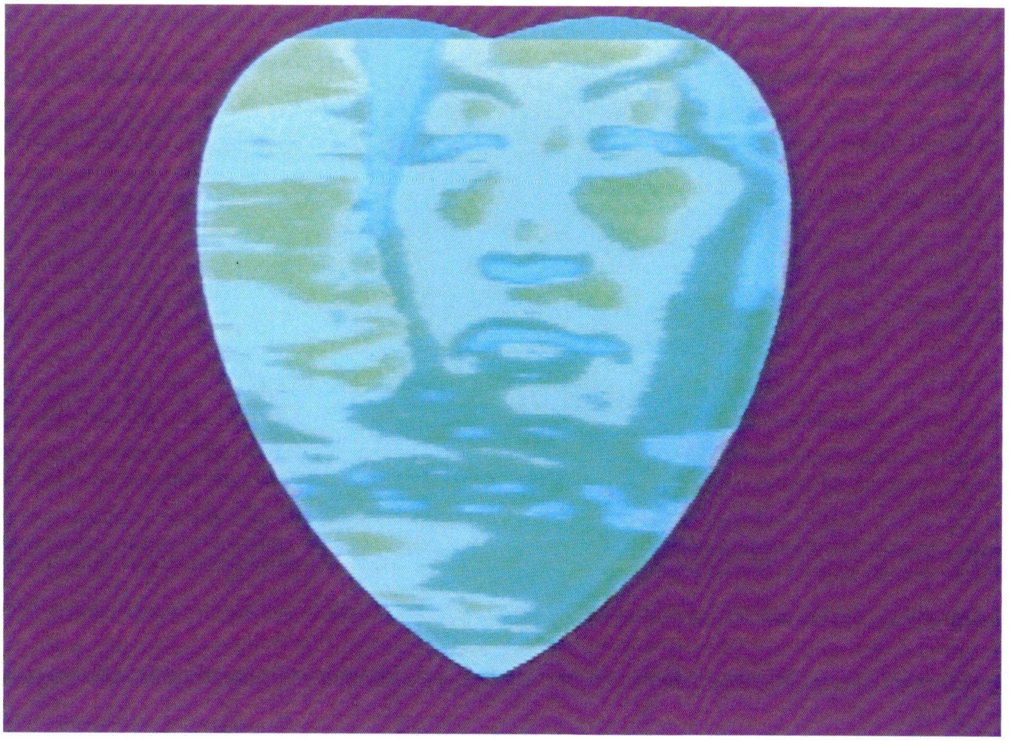
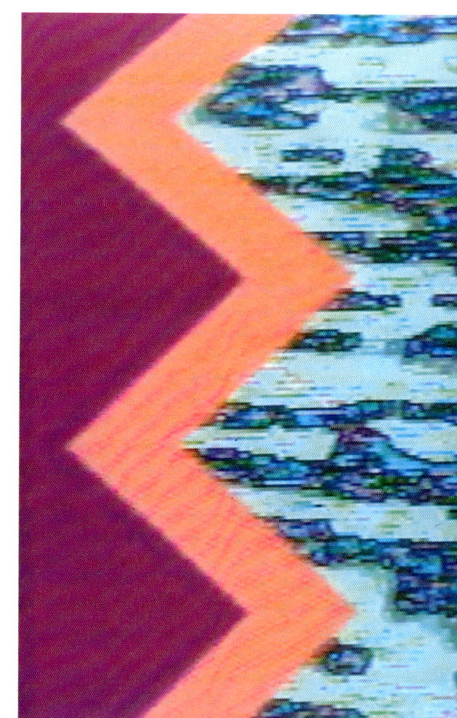

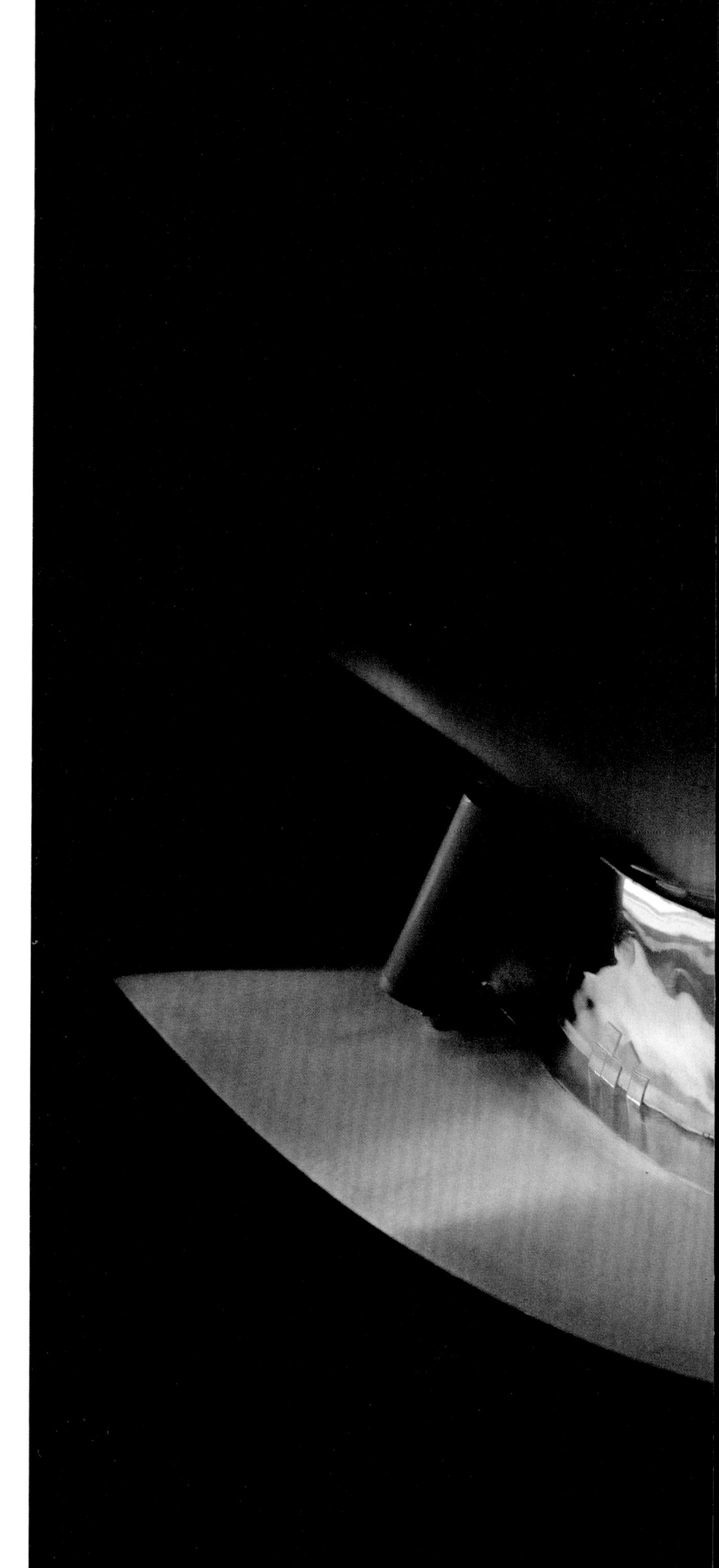

Peter Moore. Photograph of *River* installed in the Whitney Biennial, Whitney Museum of American Art, New York, March 15–May 29, 1983

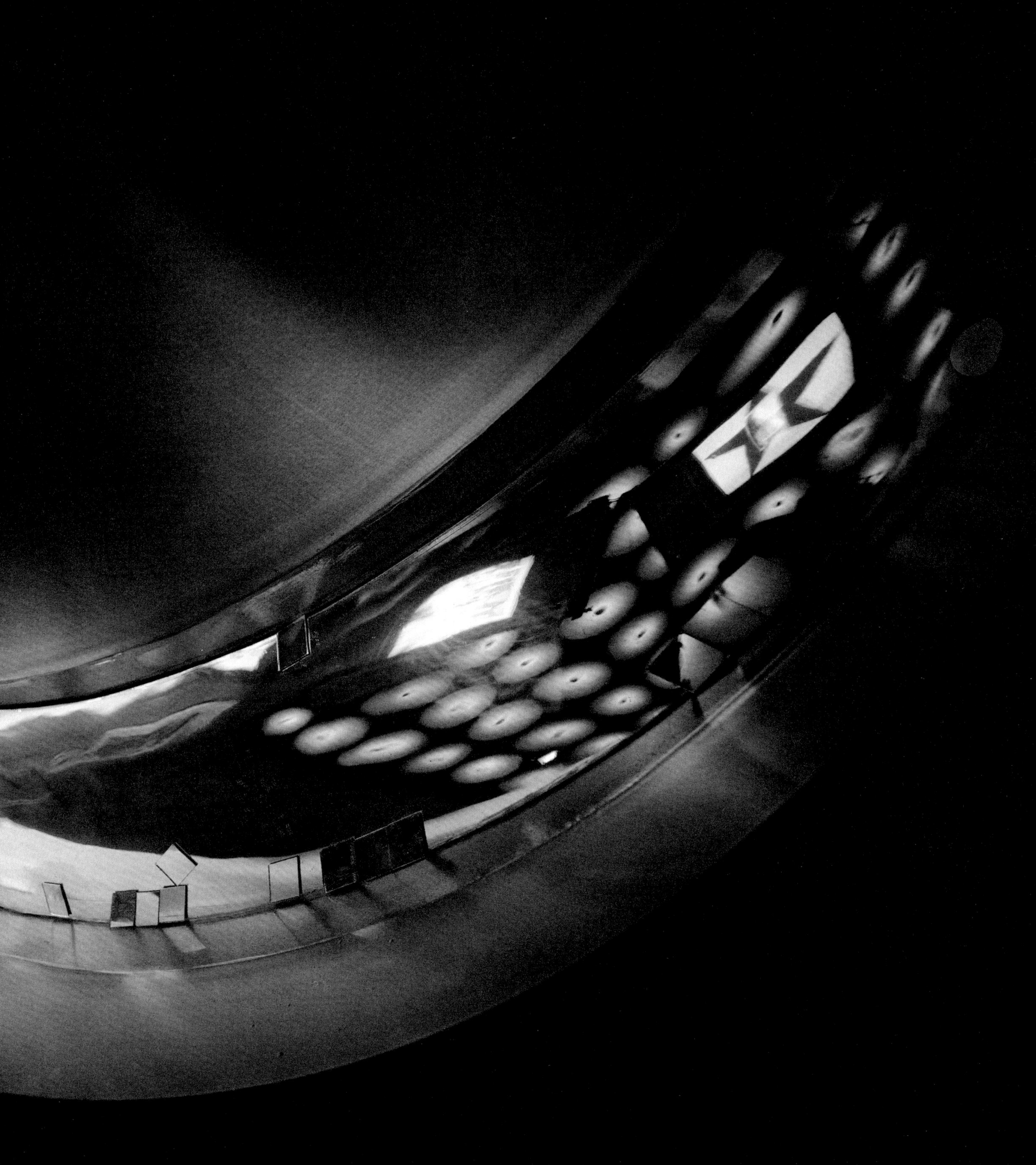

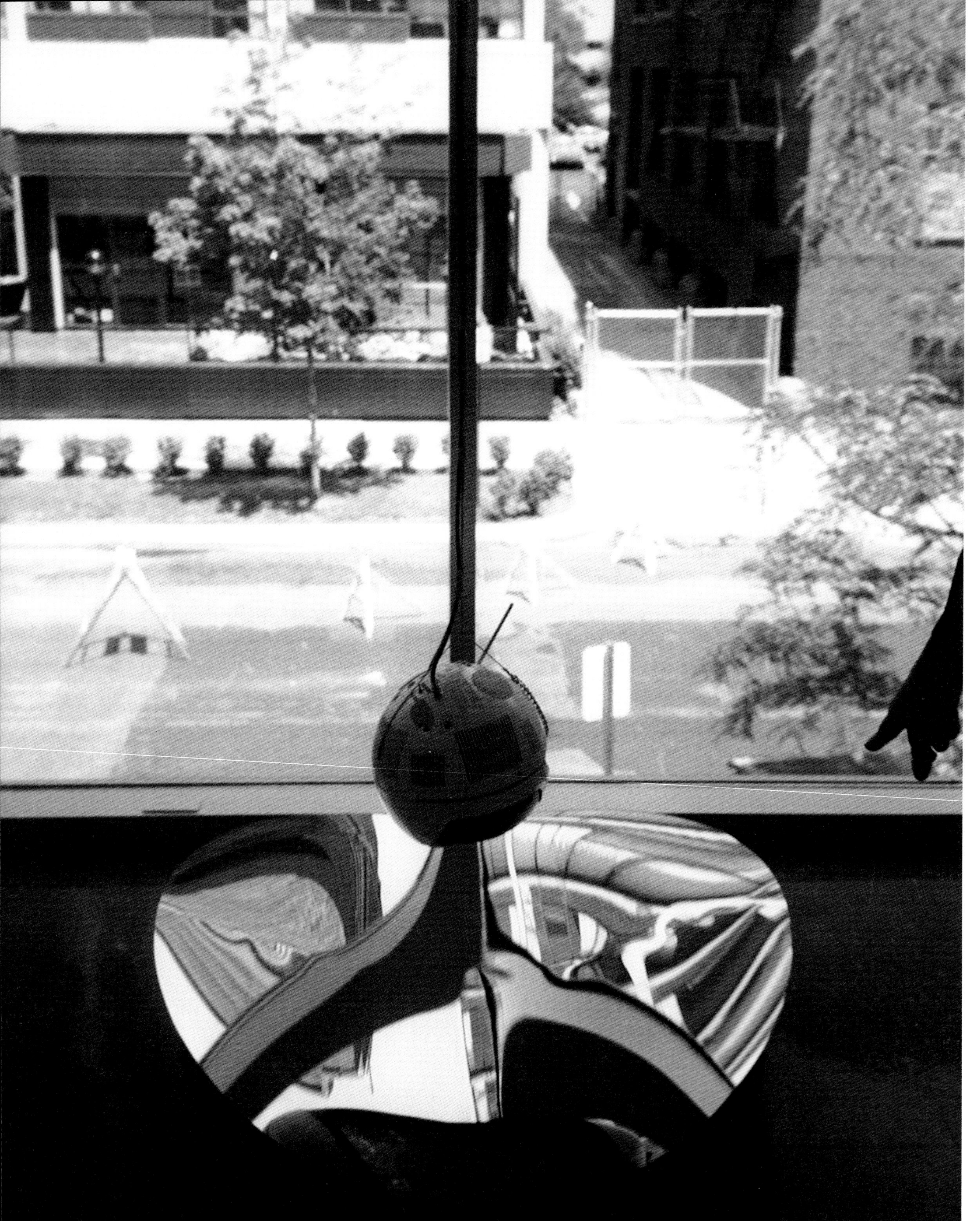

Video Haiku—Hanging Piece. 1981

Cathode-ray tube monitor, closed-circuit video camera, mirror, and plywood
Overall dimensions variable, mirror: 40 × 42 in. (101.6 × 106.7 cm)
Shigeko Kubota Video Art Foundation

Kubota frequently looked to writing and literature as sources of inspiration for her artworks and her art-making process, as seen in her early video installation *Riverrun—Video Water Poem* (1972), which borrows from James Joyce's *Finnegans Wake*; her single-channel "video diary" approach; and *Video Poem* (1970–75) (pages 38–45). With *Video Haiku—Hanging Piece*, Kubota created a visual interpretation of a haiku: a short poem that consists of a vivid depiction of a specific moment, traditionally one in nature. In contrast with *River* (1979–81) (pages 68–77) and the later *Niagara Falls I* (1985) (pages 84–91), which both integrate water, *Video Haiku* simulates a pool of water through reflections in a concave mirror sitting on the floor. Also setting this work apart is Kubota's use of closed-circuit video technology in place of recorded video content. A camera captures the work's surroundings—including the viewers present—and its signal is transmitted to a single spherical monitor hanging from the ceiling, whose screen faces down over the mirror. The slightly delayed "reflection" of the space onscreen can only be seen in the literal, real-time reflection in the mirror. The disorienting effect of these layered reflections, which seem to bend time, is intensified by the addition of a kinetic element: the suspended monitor also functions as a pendulum (powered by a motor), and the images in the mirror warp as it swings back and forth. Economical in its means, this work is one of Kubota's most direct investigations of the ways we measure and perceive time, a subject she also explored in her notebooks (fig. 1).

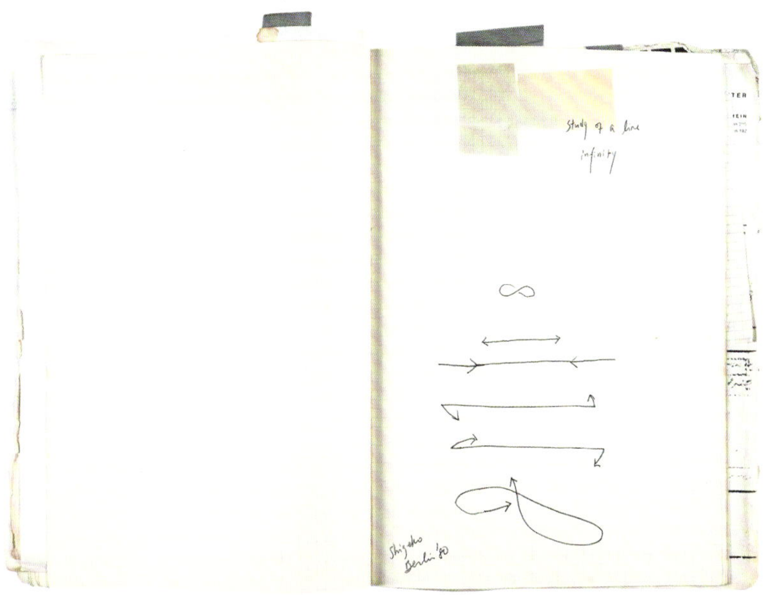

Video Haiku-Hanging Piece installed in *Options 9: Shigeko Kubota*, Museum of Contemporary Art Chicago, June 29–August 23, 1981

Fig. 1. Untitled. c. 1980. Ink on notebook paper, each page: 11 ¾ × 8 in. (29.6 × 20.3 cm). Shigeko Kubota Video Art Foundation

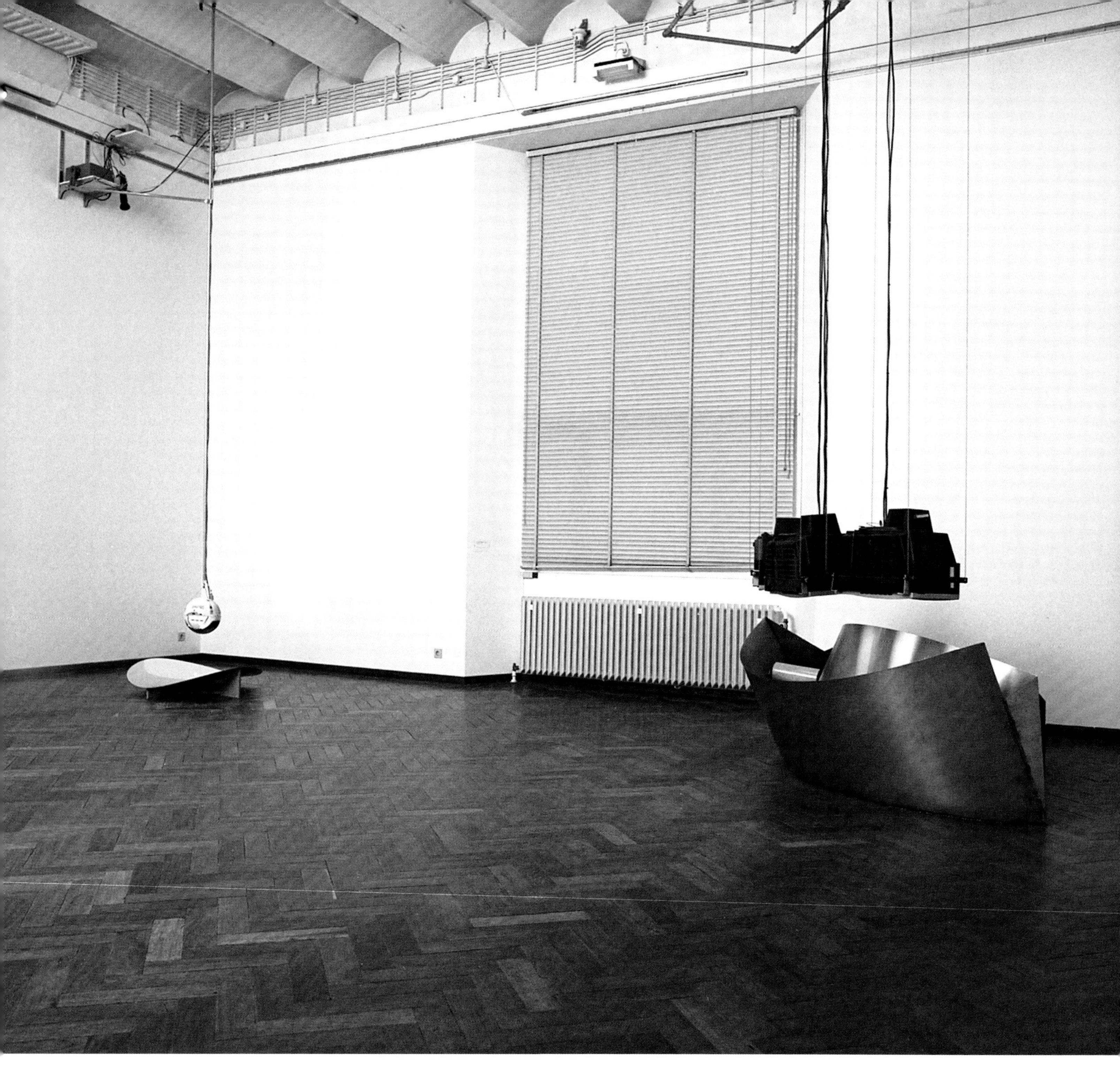

Video Haiku–Hanging Piece (left) and *River* (1979–81) installed in *Shigeko Kubota: video-sculptures 1975–1991*, Stedelijk Museum Amsterdam, October 10–November 29, 1992

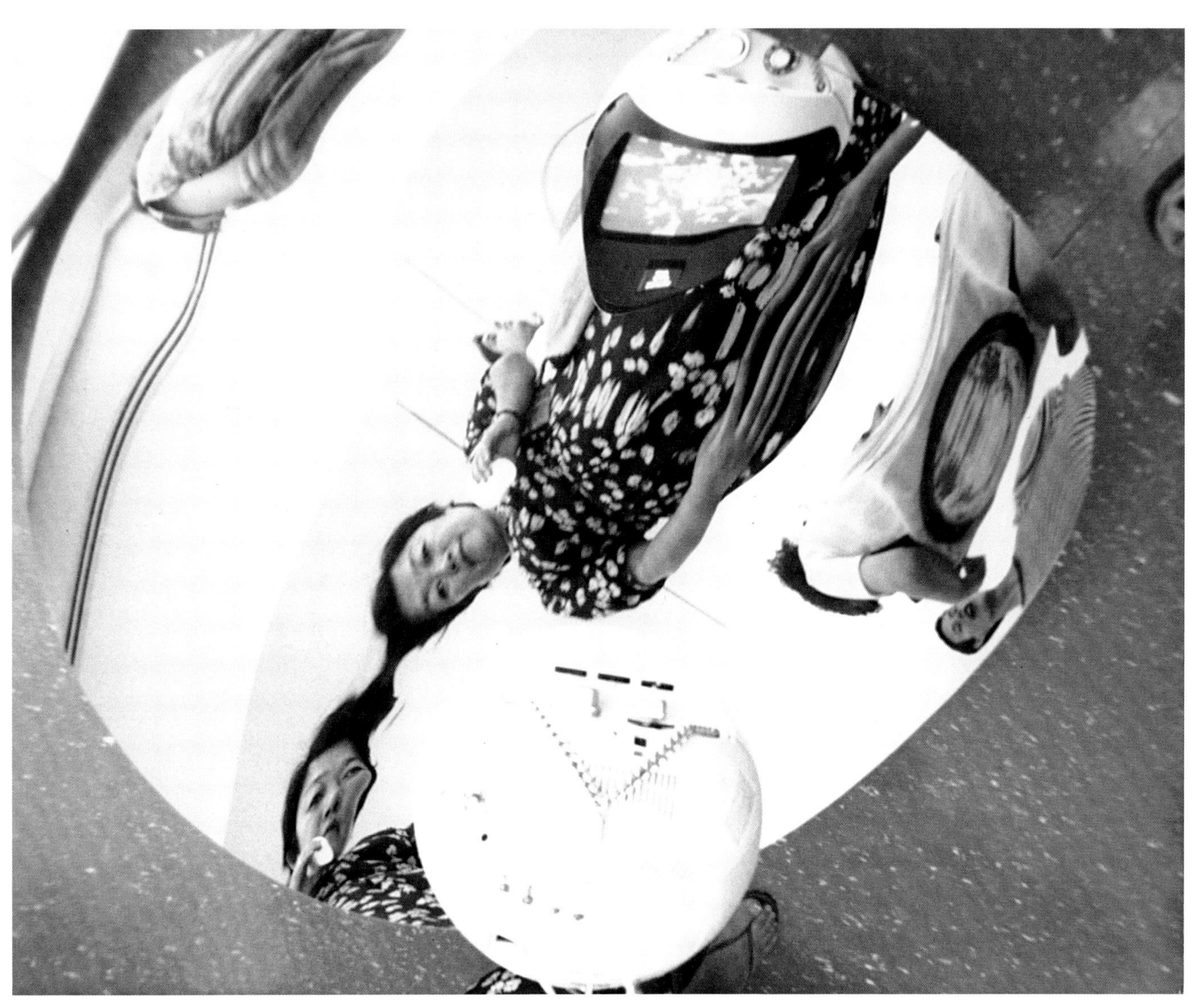

Video Haiku–Hanging Piece, with Kubota in the reflection, installed in *Options 9: Shigeko Kubota*, Museum of Contemporary Art Chicago, June 29–August 23, 1981

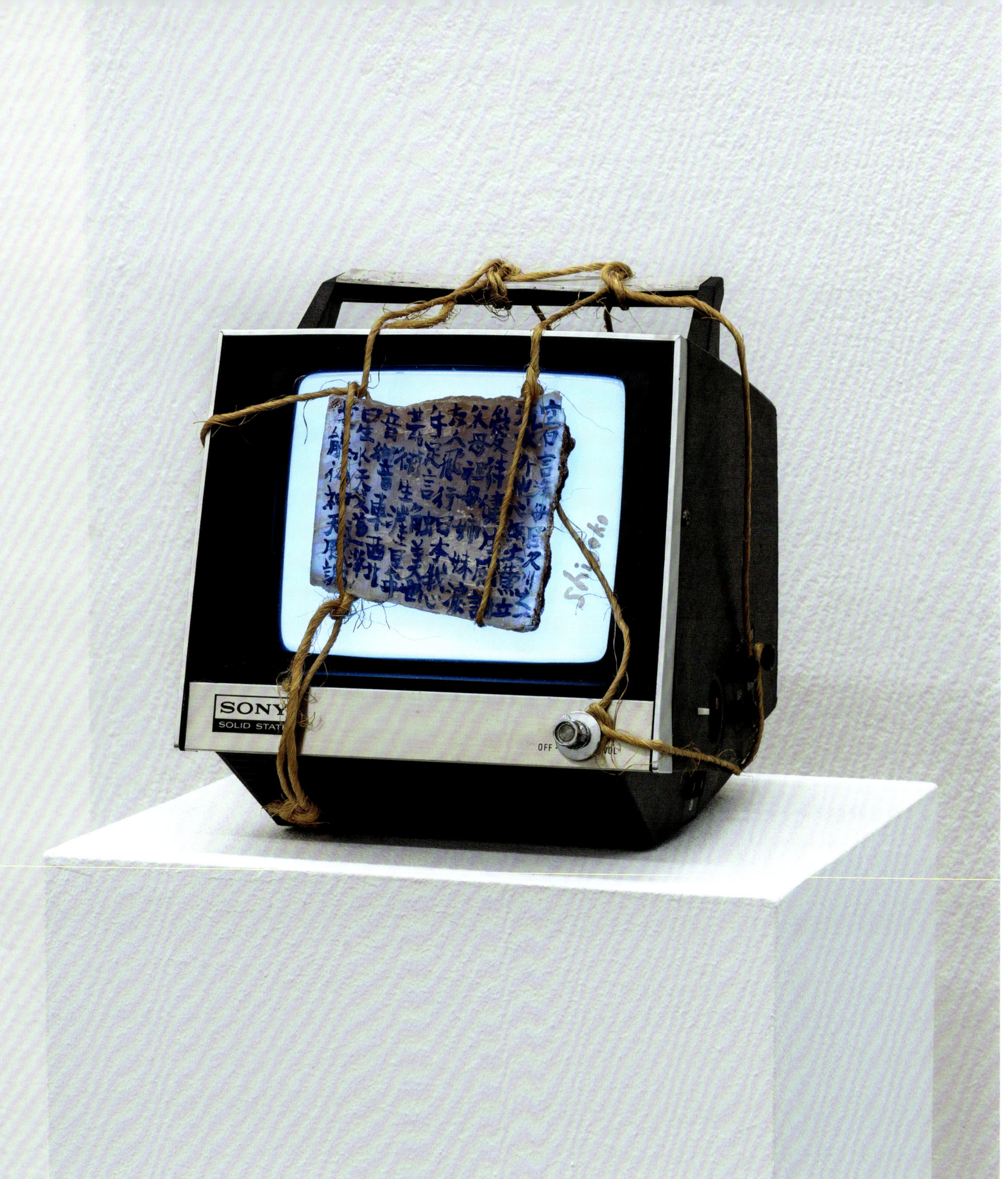

Berlin Diary: Thanks to My Ancestors installed in *flowers of sulphur*, Galerie Hubert Winter, Vienna, March 21–May 4, 2019

Berlin Diary: Thanks to My Ancestors. 1981

Cathode-ray tube monitor, crystal, ink, and twine
9 × 8 × 11 in. (22.9 × 20.3 × 27.9 cm)
The Museum of Modern Art, New York. The Modern Women's Fund, 2021

With its exposed monitor, modest scale, and handmade elements, this work stands alone in Kubota's oeuvre. Though the notion of homage is central to the Duchampiana series, this tribute is more personal. And though Kubota regularly engaged with her own identity as subject matter, *Berlin Diary: Thanks to My Ancestors*—made following a residency in Berlin hosted by the Deutscher Akademischer Austauschdienst—most directly shows her desire to reconcile her heritage with her chosen life as an international artist working at the forefront of a new medium. She inscribed the names of her ancestors on a thin sheet of pink quartz, which she then affixed to a small television using a piece of twine. The appearance of her own handwriting, rare in her sculpture, combined with a remnant of the natural world, imbues the television with a talismanic quality. To adopt a term Kubota used in reference to another video sculpture, *Berlin Diary* can be viewed as her most quintessential "autobiographical object."[1] Her calligraphy, illuminated by the electric glow of the monitor screen, performs the role of the personal images that populate her single-channel video diaries. Her use of assemblage—as if a piece of twine could physically bind her personal history with video technology—shows her searching for a new visual language, to deeply moving and strikingly poetic effect. This work also points to Kubota's interest in the relationship between video, death, and memory, which she traced back to her upbringing in a monastic Buddhist family. In her writings Kubota contemplated video as an "extension of the brain's memory cells"[2] or even a form of communication with the dead; by illuminating the names of her ancestors she created a work that fits her definition of video as a "living altar."[3]

1 This phrase is written on a sketch for *Three Mountains* (reproduced on page 16 of the present volume).
2 Kubota, "Video Sculpture: Two Phases," in Zdenek Felix, ed., *Shigeko Kubota: Video Sculptures*, exh. cat. (Berlin: Daadgalerie; Essen: Museum Folkwang; Zurich: Kunsthaus Zürich, 1981), 13.
3 Ibid.

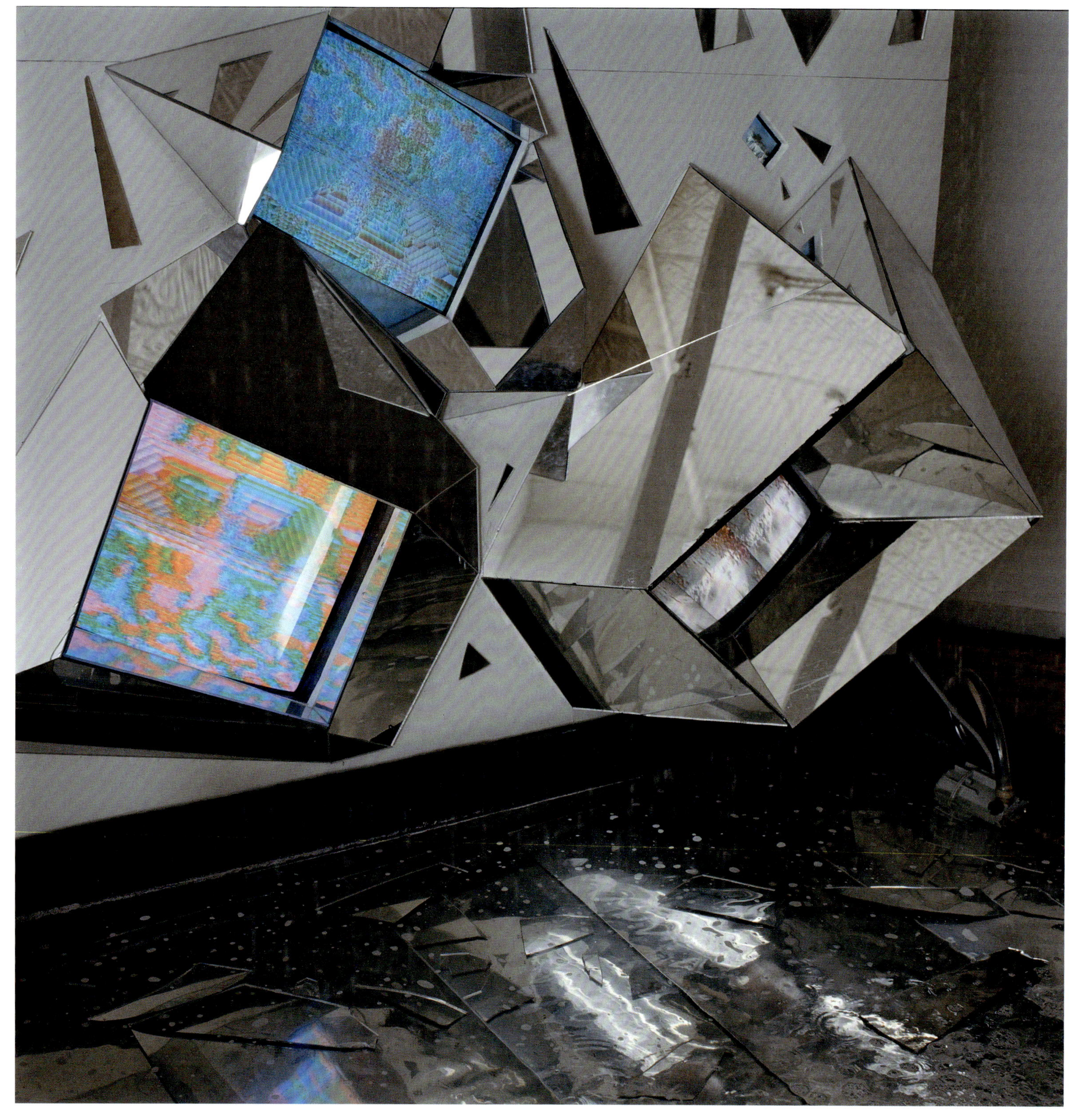

Peter Moore. Photograph of *Niagara Falls I* installed in *Niagara Falls: Summer, Fall, and Winter*, The Kitchen, New York, March 9–30, 1985

Niagara Falls I. 1985

Four-channel standard-definition video (color, sound; approx. 31 min. each), ten cathode-ray tube monitors, plastic mirrors, plywood, water, and sprinkler system
8 ft. × 54 in. × 8 ft. (243.8 × 137.2 × 243.8 cm)
Constructed by Kevin Johnson
Shigeko Kubota Video Art Foundation

"Beauty of nature is nightmare, fear, and terror," Kubota wrote of this work in 1991. "Niagara Falls particularly, because of its magnetic force of nature, plunges into my impulse to thrust myself to death. . . . Niagara Falls has a particular kind of beauty that makes you feel liberated from yourself."[1] Here absolute freedom is equated with the potential of self-obliteration. In its totemic scale and harsh geometry, *Niagara Falls I* is a gothic tribute to the elemental—that which connected landscape, death, and video throughout Kubota's oeuvre.[2] Kubota initially shot the falls at the precipice with the assistance of friends and collaborators Paul Garrin and Vernon Norwood, who held onto a belt tied around her waist so that she wouldn't fall in.[3] In the resulting sculpture, an ad hoc frame supports a relief made of plywood and mirrors that is suggestive of a waterfall, with cascading movement conveyed by screens of varying sizes arranged in Cubist fashion. The four video channels that make up this collage—each captured in a different season, with the one from summer featuring the roaring sounds of water—have been processed and reprocessed, at times beyond recognition; lush close-ups, which transmit the sensation of being consumed by the falls,[4] are further obfuscated by a curtain of water generated by a self-contained pump system. One of the video channels is also projected onto the sculpture, heightening the viewer's sense of disorientation. Reflected in the mirrors, the projection rhymes with the images emanating from the monitors; captured in the water droplets, it produces a flickering effect that contrasts with the rigid forms of the sculptural backdrop. At the base of the sculpture, a basin filled with water and mirror fragments collects the work's many layers of images.

1 Kubota, in Mary Jane Jacob, ed., *Shigeko Kubota Video Sculpture* (New York: American Museum of the Moving Image, 1991), 55.
2 "In Buddhism after we die we will become dust," she wrote. "We become part of the earth. Very elemental. But even Yves Klein, French artist, said art is ash of art. Art is ash of yourself. But Buddhists are always coming to the ashes. So I like landscape, where coming to the art is more elemental." Kubota, in Jeanine Mellinger and D. L. Bean, "Shigeko Kubota," *Profile* 3, no. 6 (November–December 1983): 19; quoted in Emily Watlington, "Total Freedom to Dissolve," *Haunt Journal of Art* 4 (October 2017): 15.
3 Jacob, *Shigeko Kubota Video Sculpture*, 55.
4 Watlington's reading of Kubota's use of close-up images informed this description. See Watlington, "Total Freedom to Dissolve," 16.

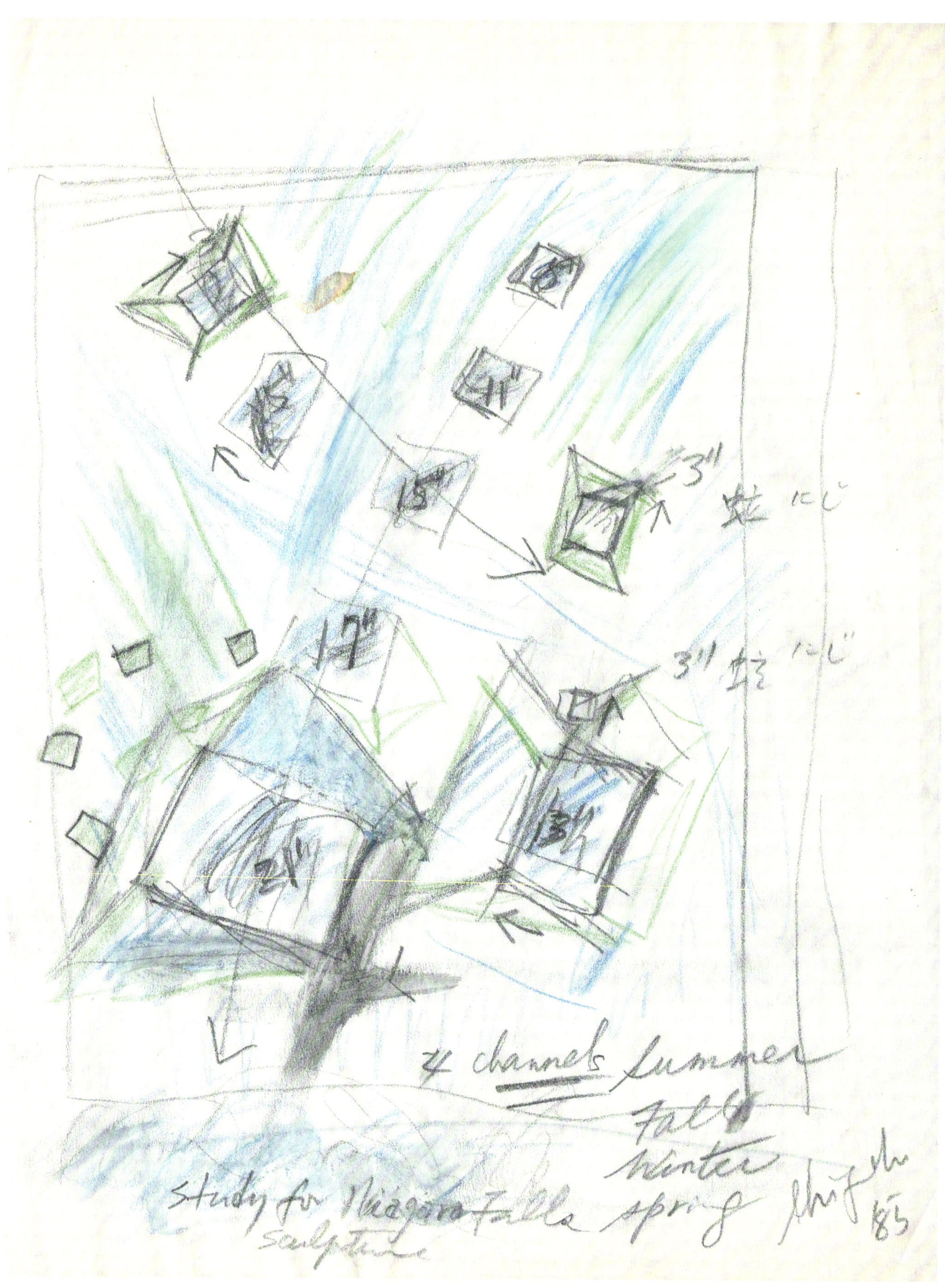

Study for *Niagara Falls I*. 1985. Graphite and colored pencil on paper, 11 × 8 ½ in. (27.9 × 21.6 cm). Shigeko Kubota Video Art Foundation

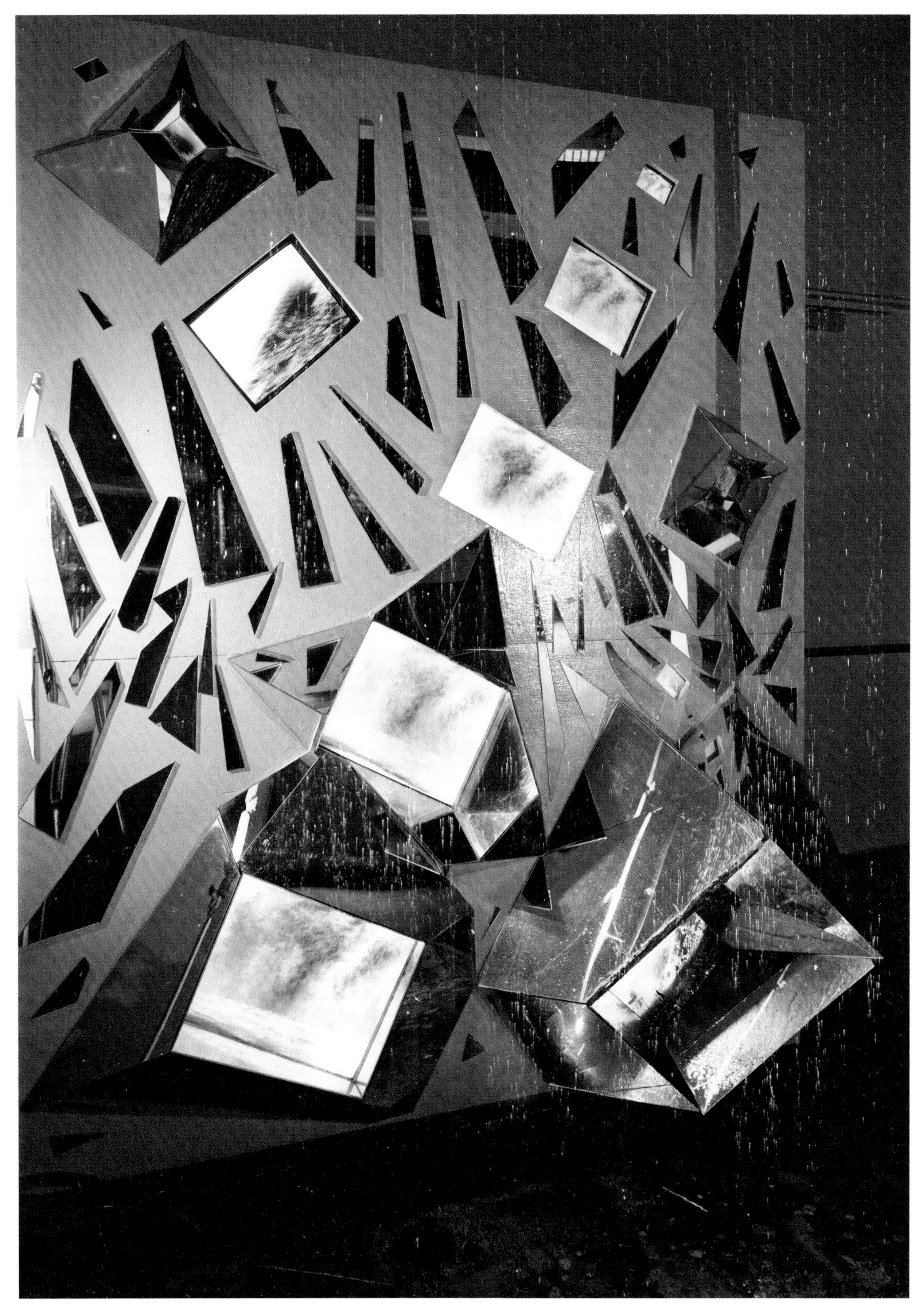

Peter Moore. Photograph of *Niagara Falls I* installed in *Shigeko Kubota Video Sculpture,* American Museum of the Moving Image, New York, April 26–September 15, 1991

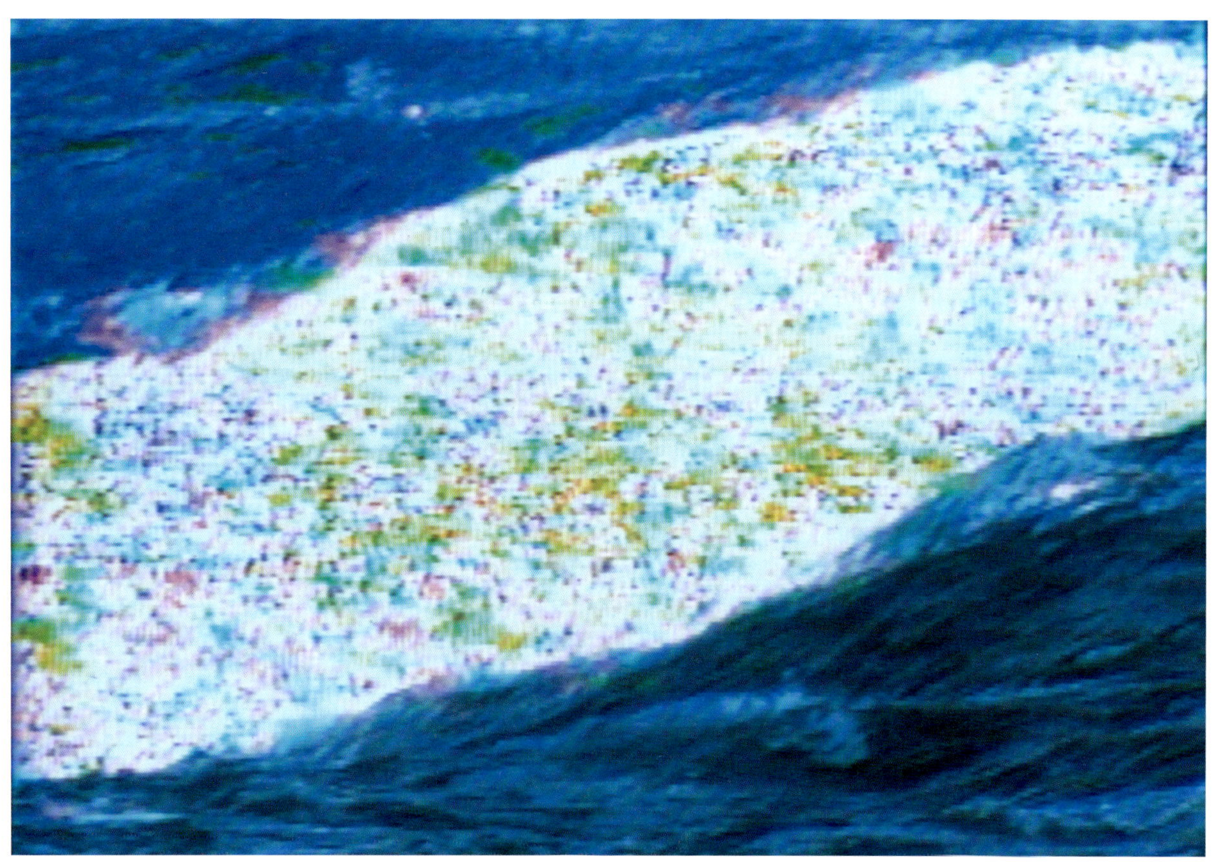

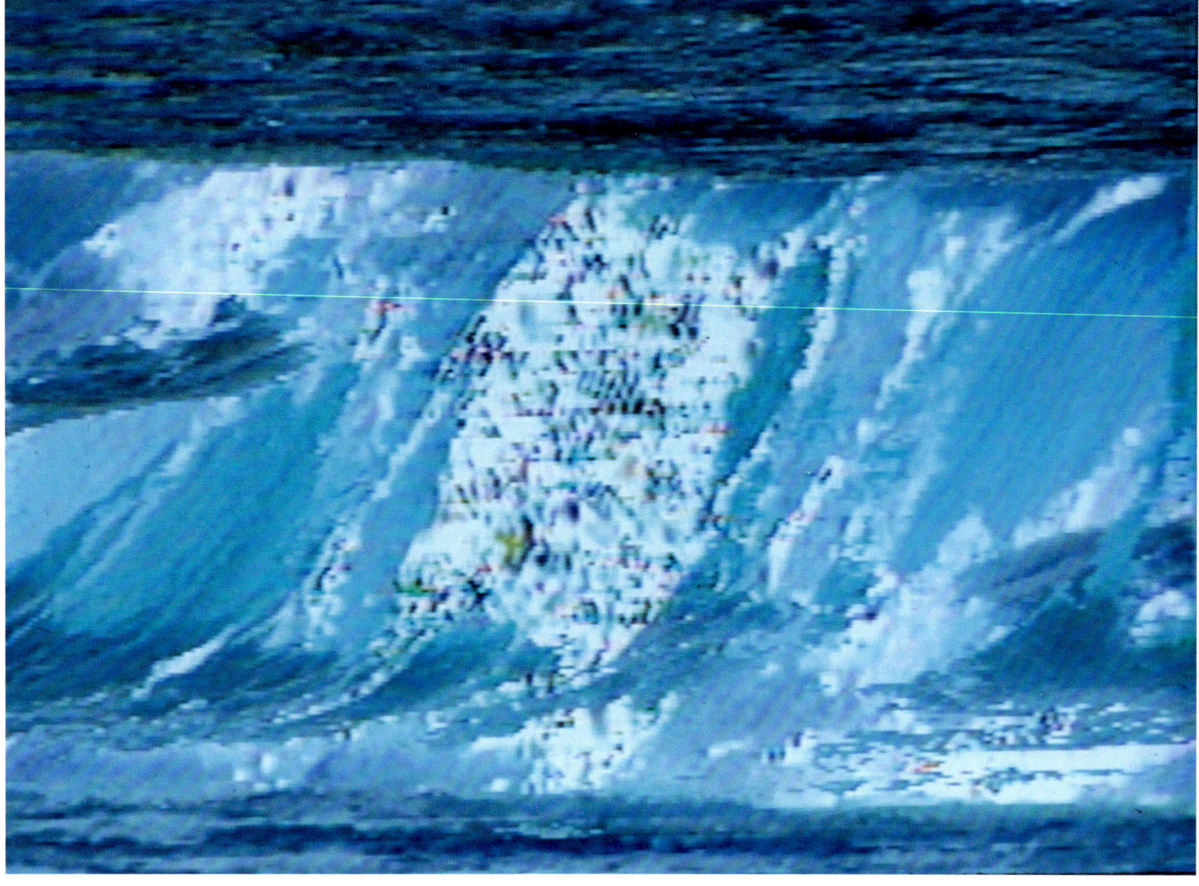

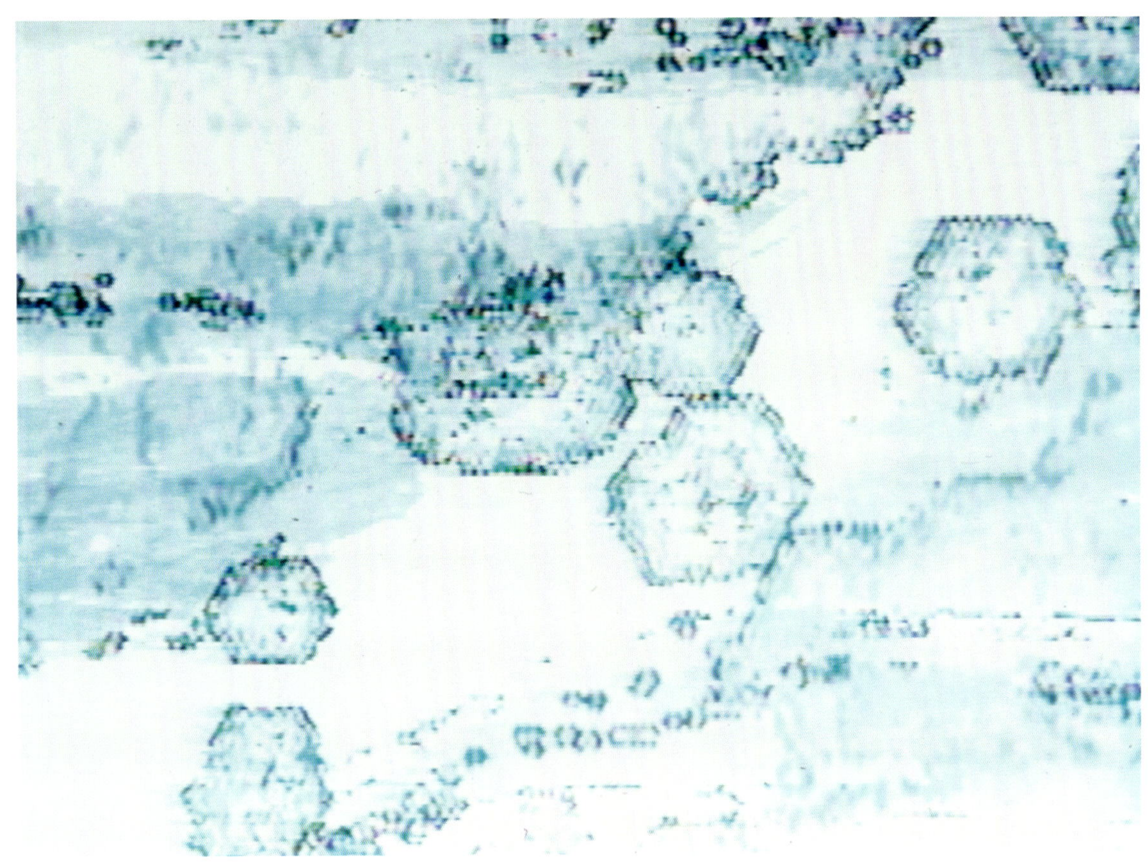

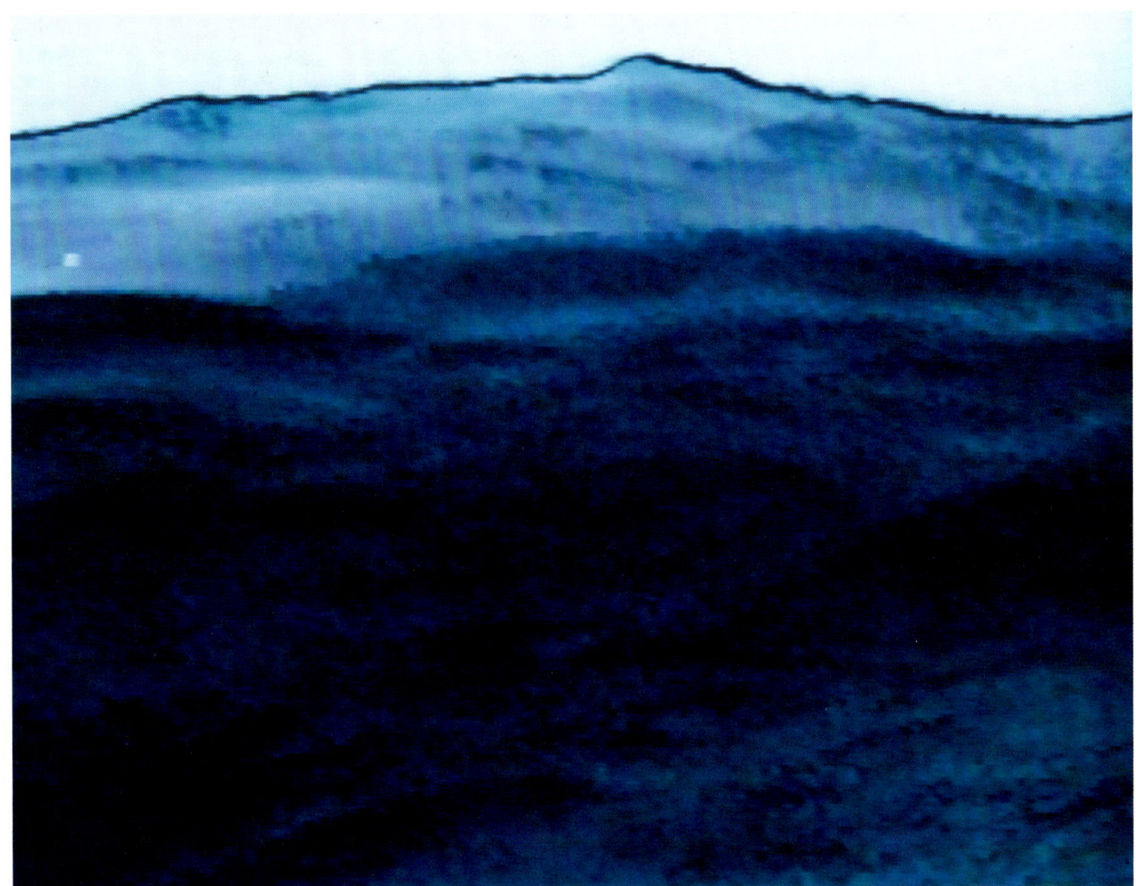

 Stills from *Niagara Falls I*

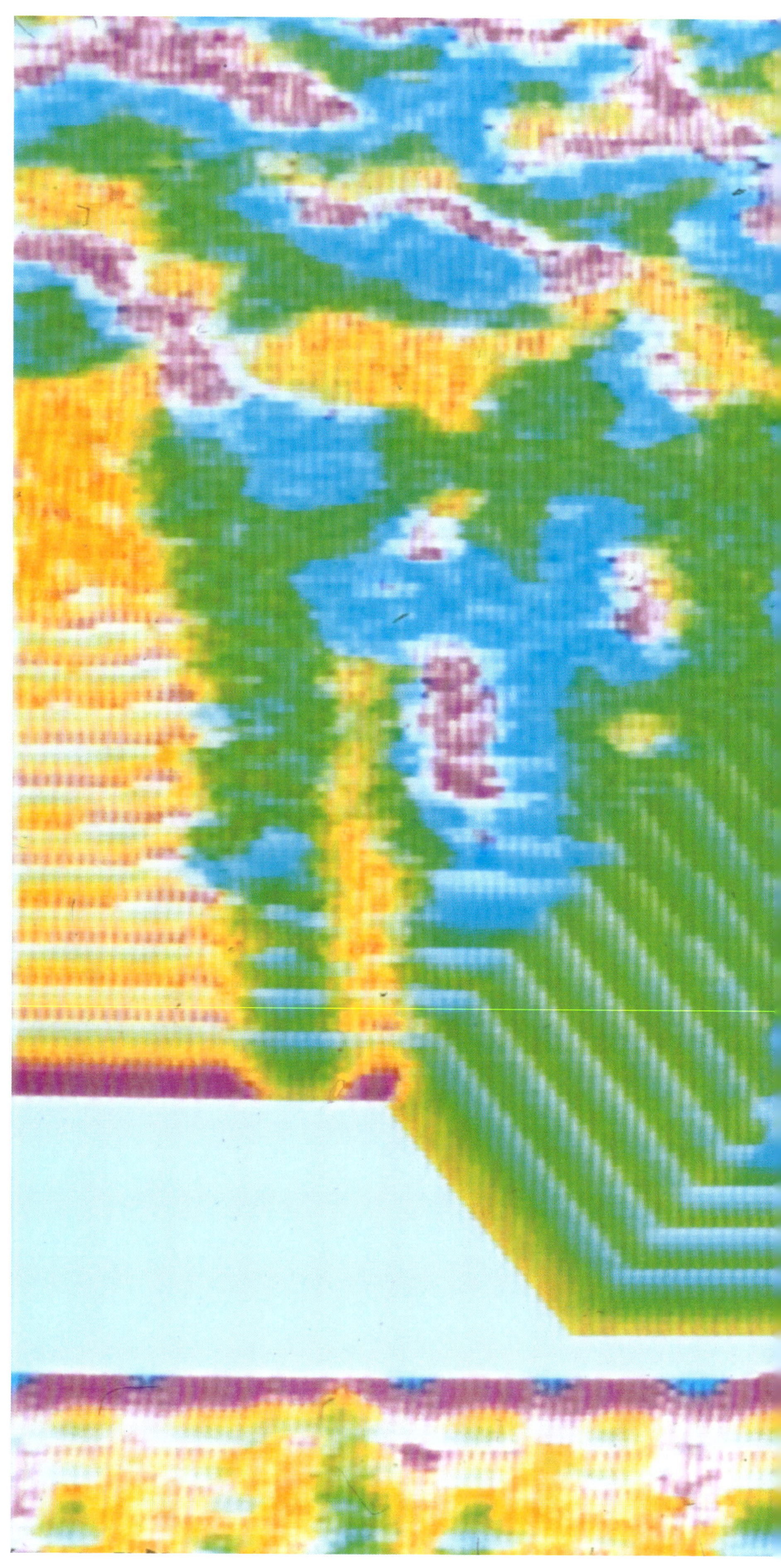

Still from *Niagara Falls I*

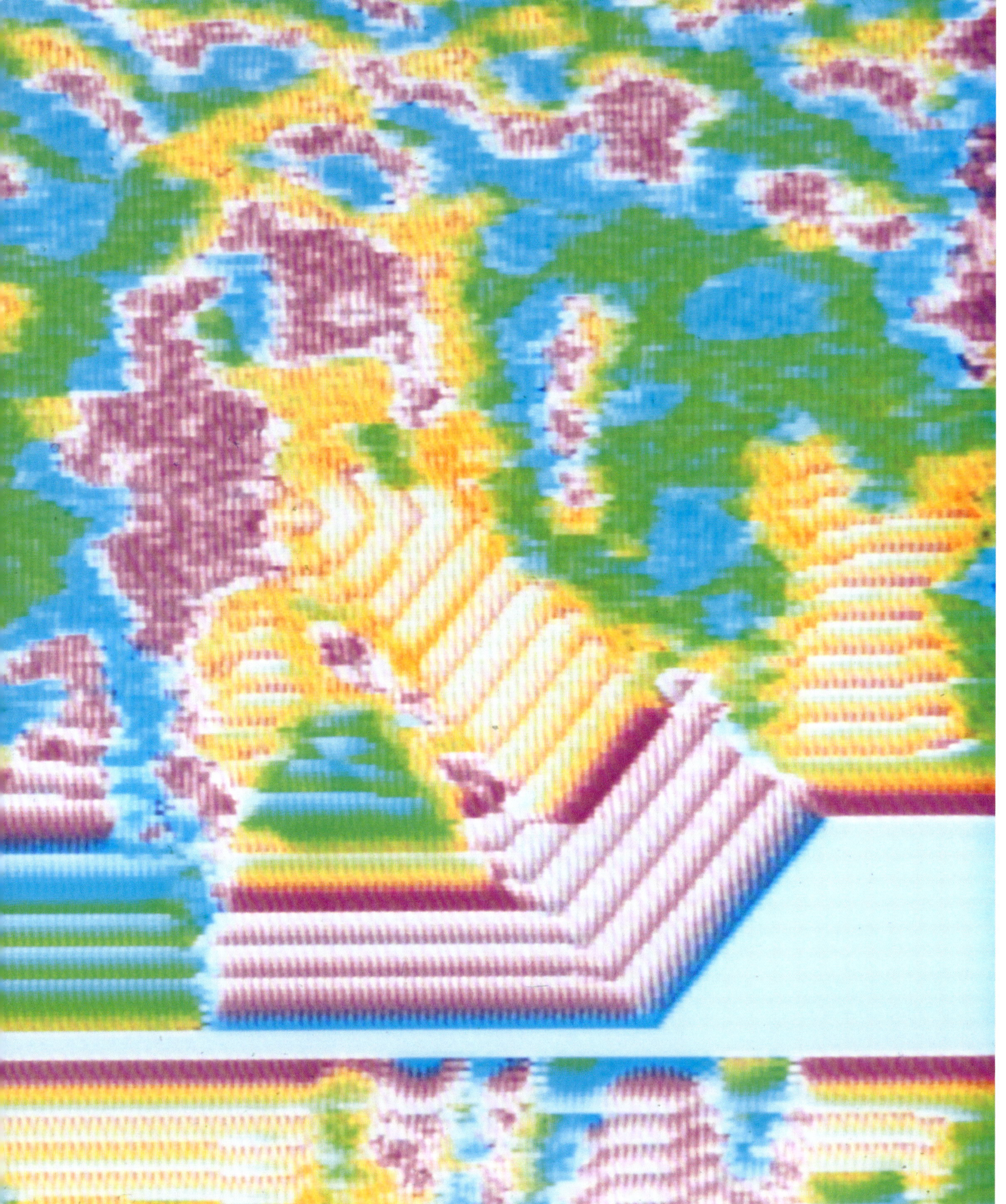

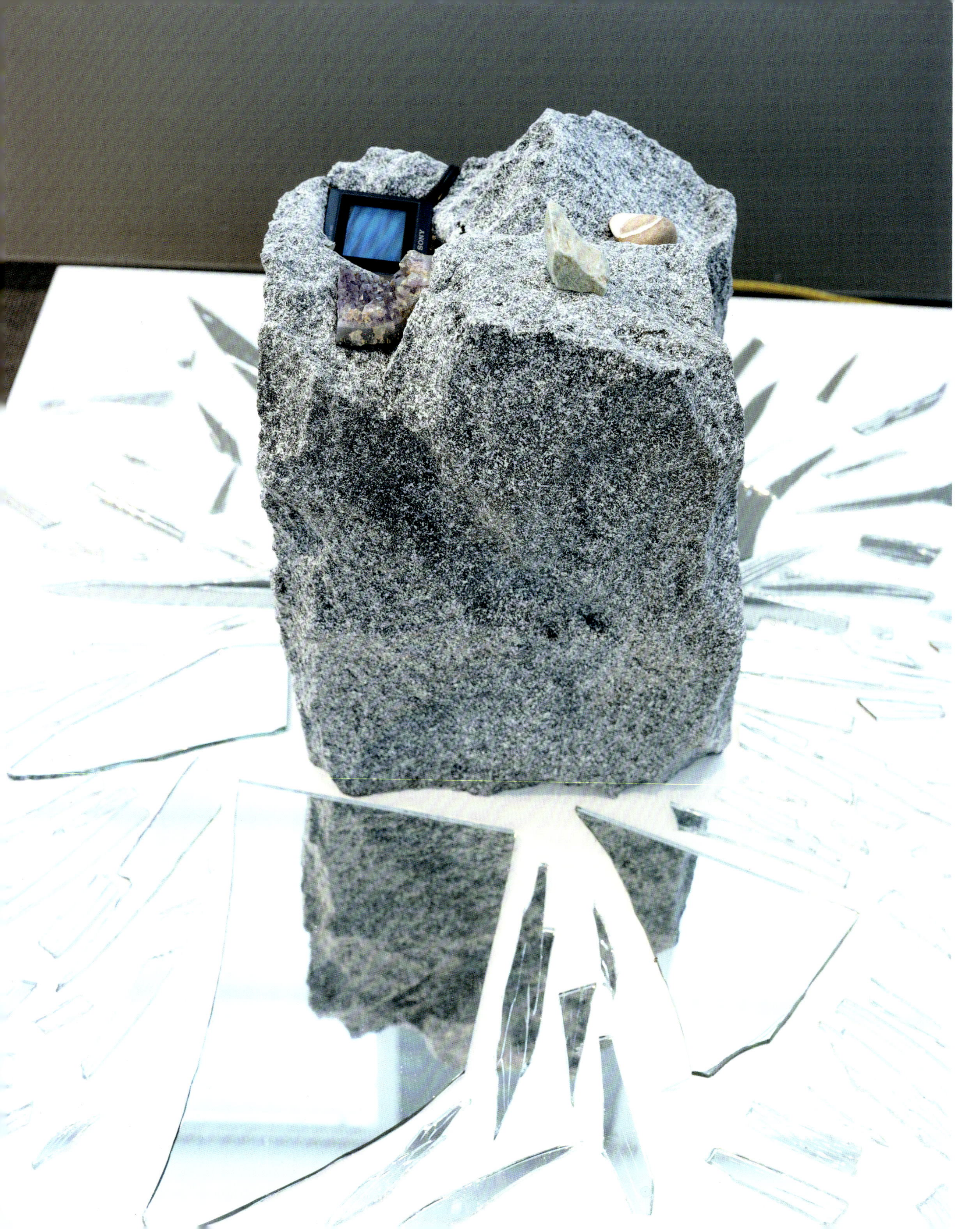
SONY

Rock Video Cherry Blossom. 1986

Standard-definition video (color, silent; 12:54 min.), LCD monitor, foam rubber, paint, stones, geode, and mirror shards
16 × 24 × 16 in. (40.6 × 61 × 40.6 cm)
Shigeko Kubota Video Art Foundation

This work is not in the exhibition.

In a departure from Kubota's earlier plywood and metal sculptures, this work—in which a monitor and a handful of stones and crystals are affixed to a replica of a rock—engages the sculptural tradition of assemblage. It also references Japanese rock gardens, "dry landscapes" meant to represent natural scenes, including mountains and water, and to foster meditation.[1] Kubota's decision to imitate a heavy rock using a light, synthetic foam is just one of the poetic contradictions in this work. The five-inch monitor is similar in scale to the rocks and geode and is nestled into the larger form in the same way, suggesting a correspondence between the slowness of geological time and the speed of modern technology. Yet the contrast between these disparate elements is also emphasized by the overt presence of the technological apparatus; rather than being concealed as in Kubota's other works, the monitor's face plate is exposed, and its power cable is conspicuous. This early model of a liquid-crystal-display (LCD) monitor did not generate a lot of heat, unlike the cathode-ray tube monitors the artist had used until this point, and so it could be placed directly against the foam rather than in a compartment with a fan. The video depicts cherry blossoms—which appear elsewhere in Kubota's oeuvre, including the spring channel of *Niagara Falls I* (pages 84–91)—that have been rigorously abstracted into pulsating fractals, warped, tiled, and turned inside out. The riotous, kaleidoscopic nature of these images is enhanced by their juxtaposition with the motionless rock, which was initially surrounded by mirror shards—arranged as if shattered under its weight—and, later, a layer of gravel as well (fig. 1).

1 Thanks to Lia Robinson of the Shigeko Kubota Video Art Foundation for her insights on this point.

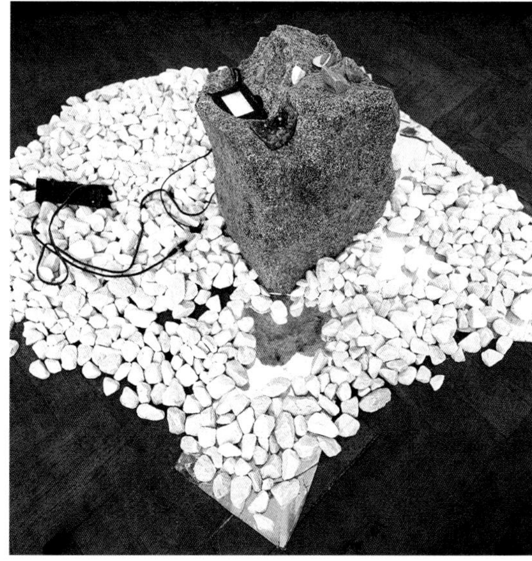

Fig. 1. *Rock Video Cherry Blossom* installed in *Shigeko Kubota: video-sculptures 1975–1991*, Stedelijk Museum Amsterdam, October 10–November 29, 1992

Peter Moore. Photograph of *Rock Video Cherry Blossom* installed in *Shigeko Kubota Video Sculpture*, American Museum of the Moving Image, New York, April 26–September 15, 1991

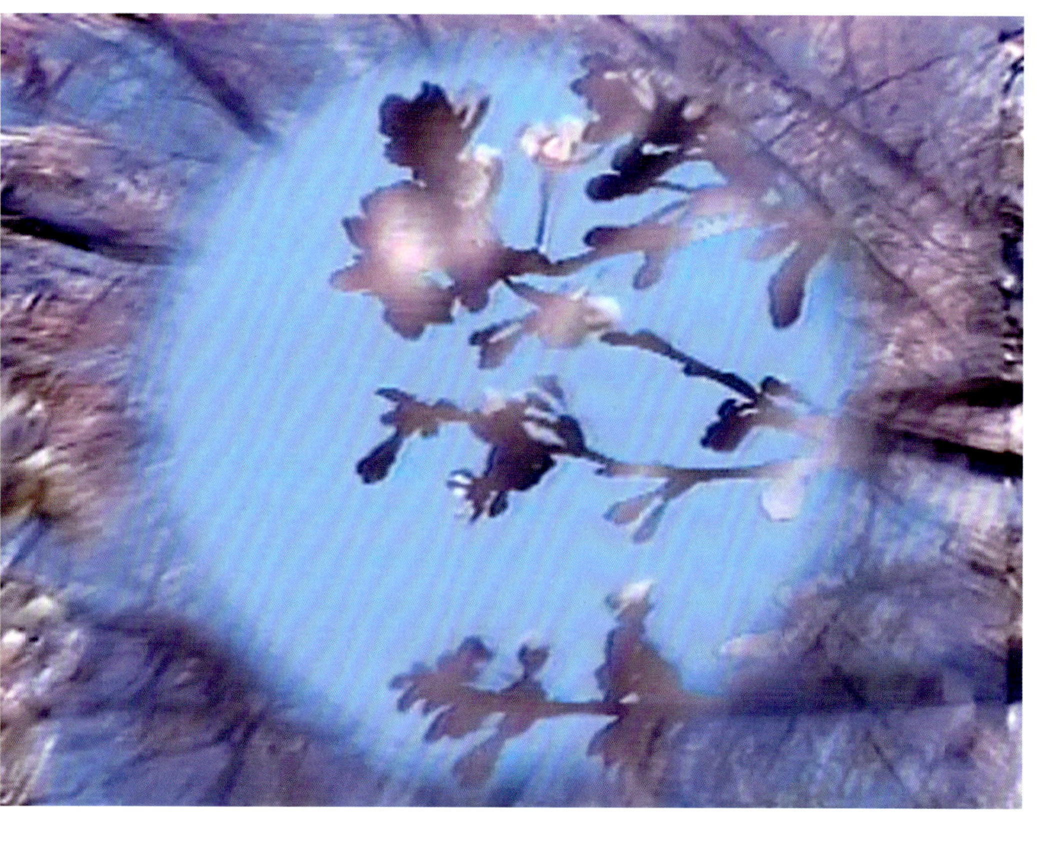

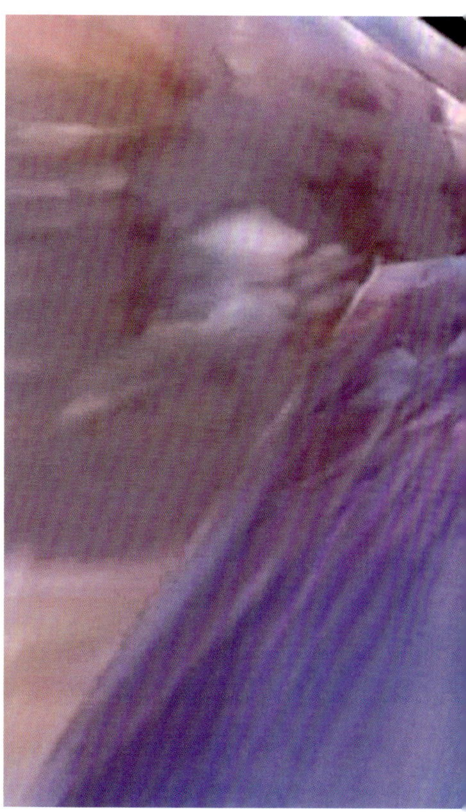

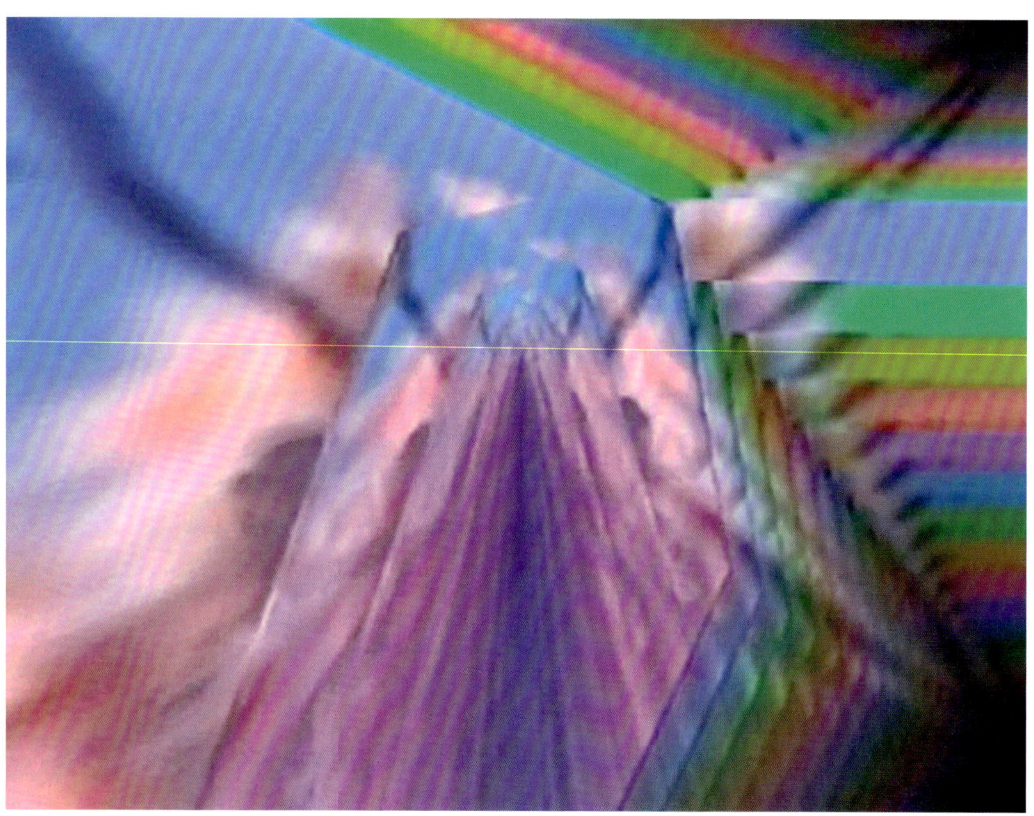

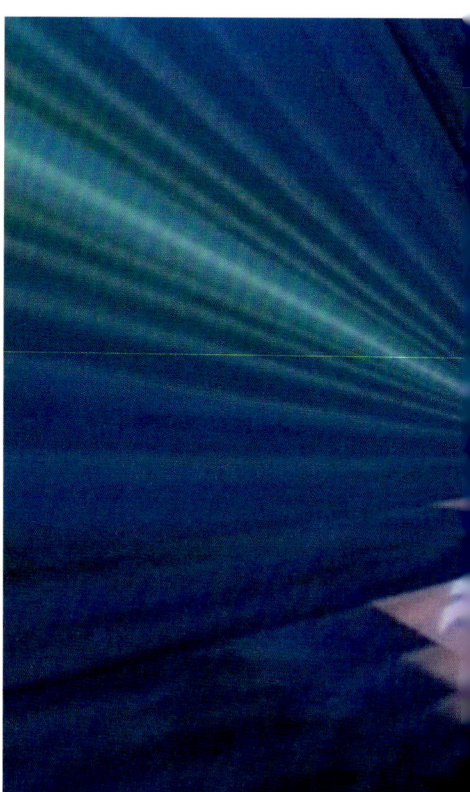

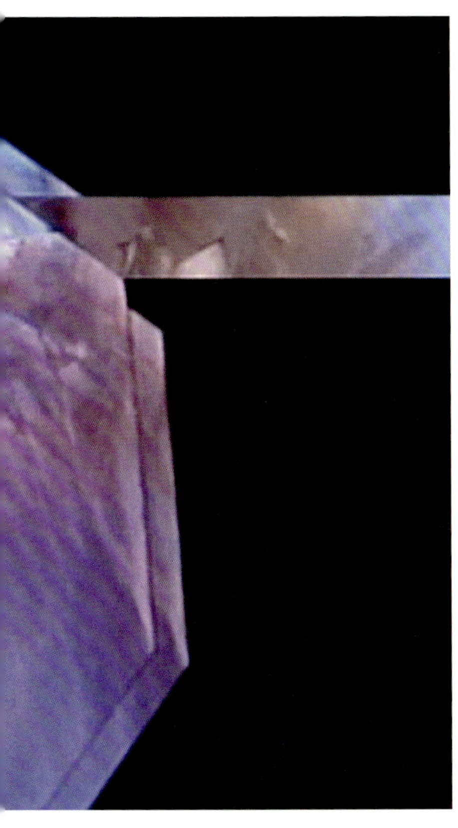
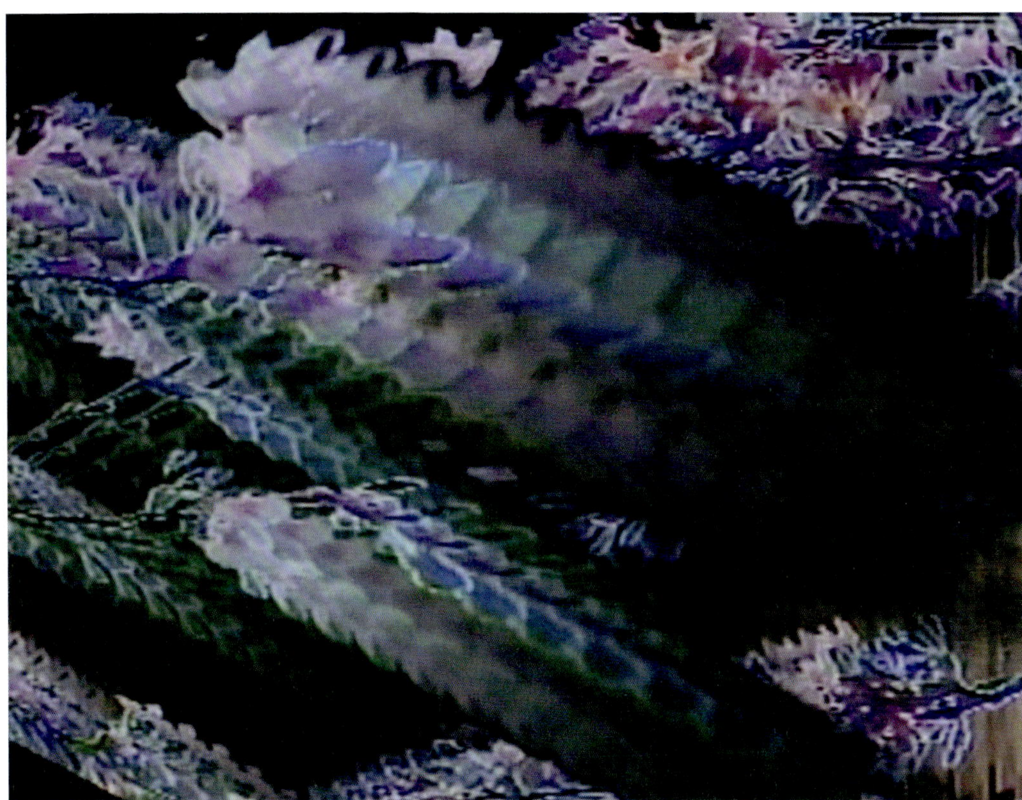
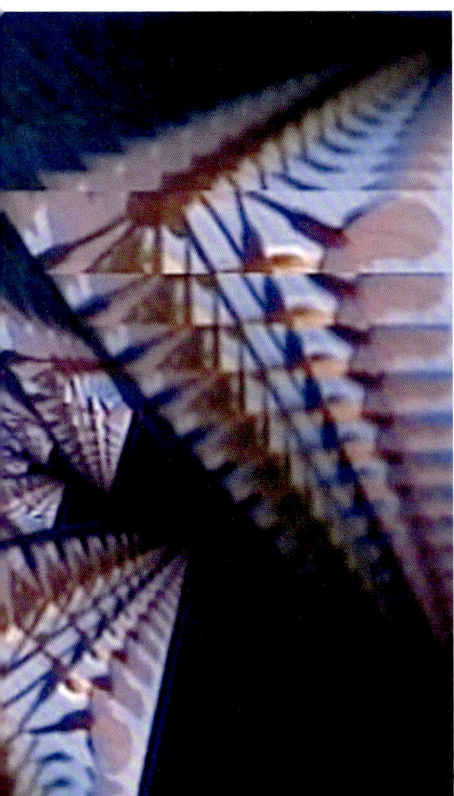
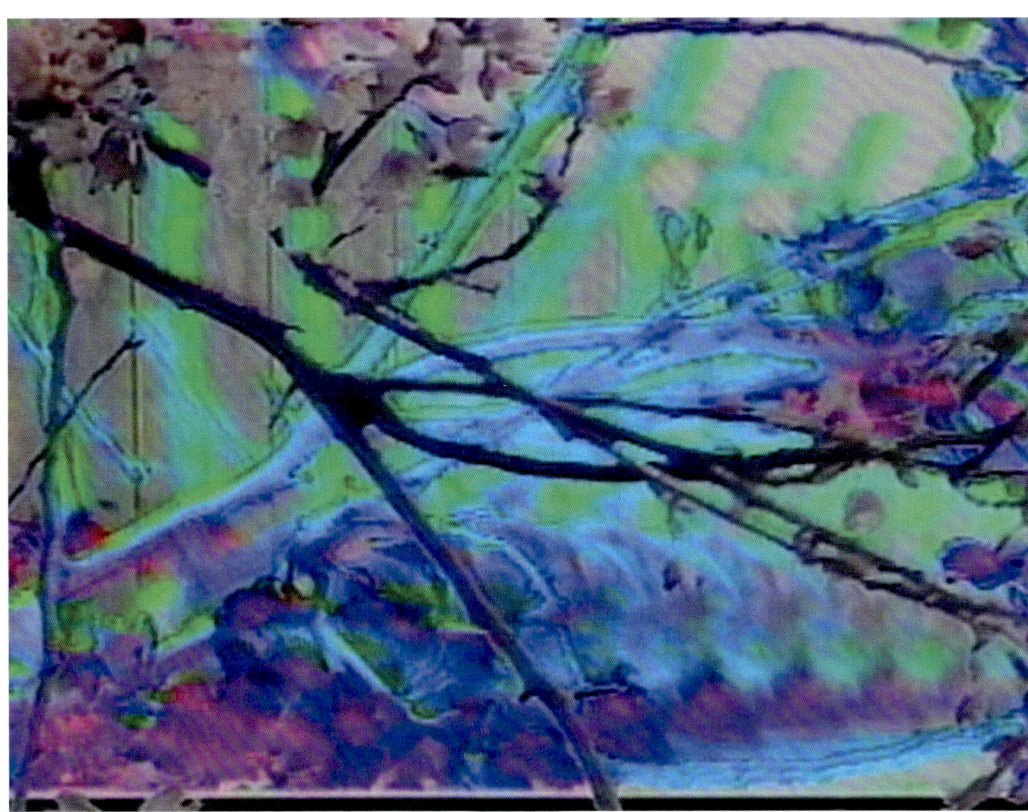

Stills from *Rock Video Cherry Blossom*

Watercolor diary. 1988

Each page: 6 × 4 in. (15.2 × 10.2 cm)
Shigeko Kubota Video Art Foundation

This work is not in the exhibition.

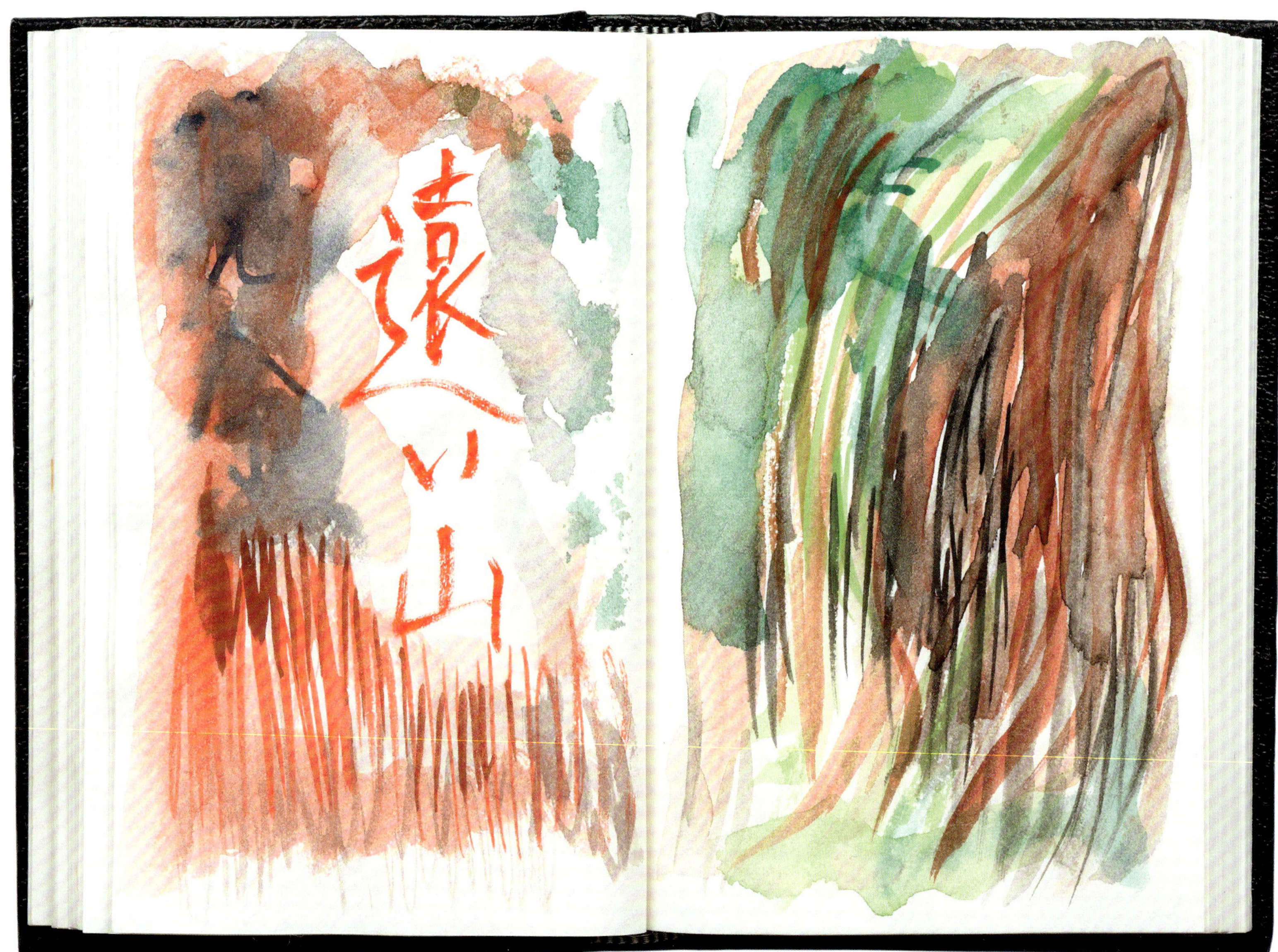

Distant mountain

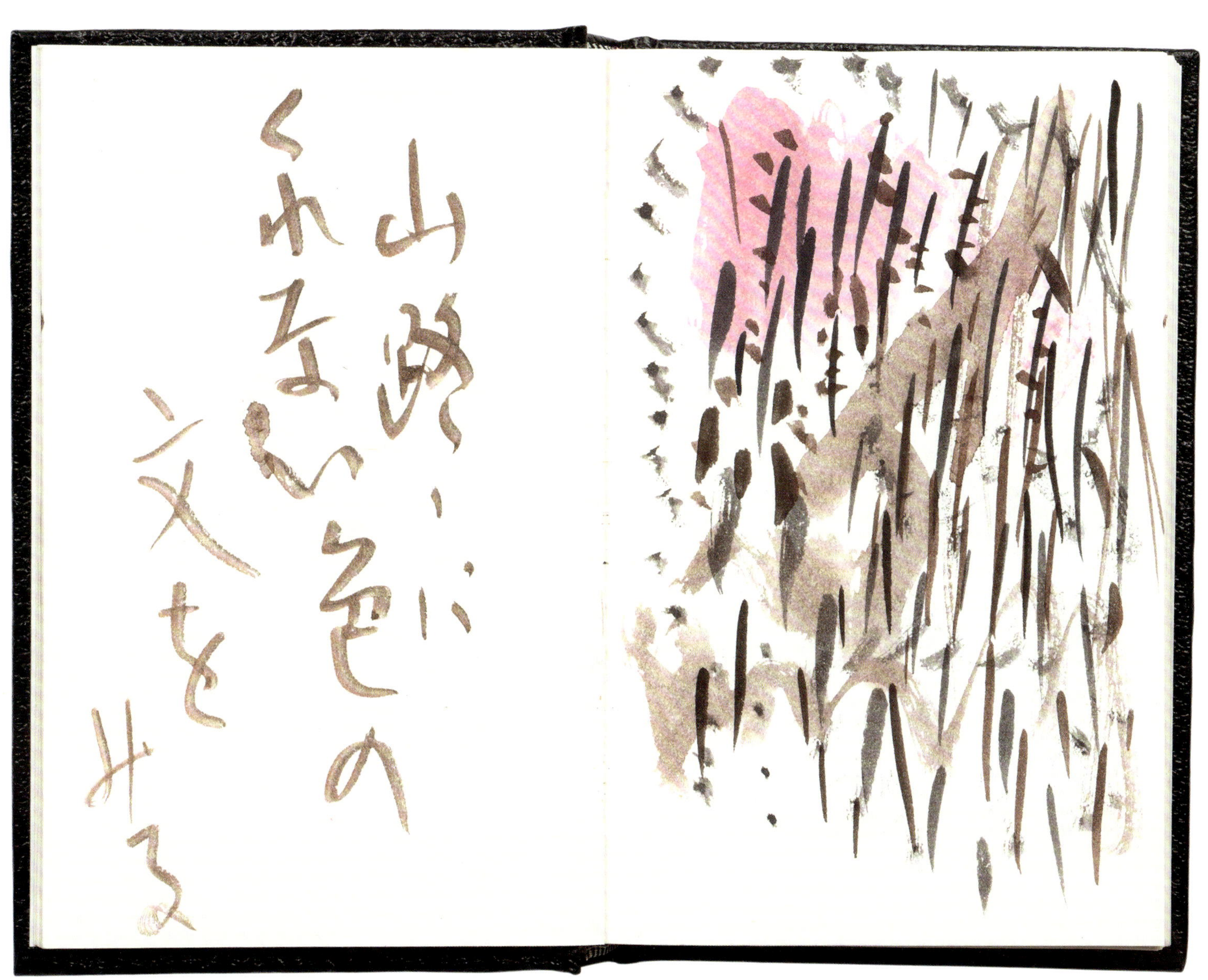

On the mountain path
Viewing the crimson-colored
patterns before me

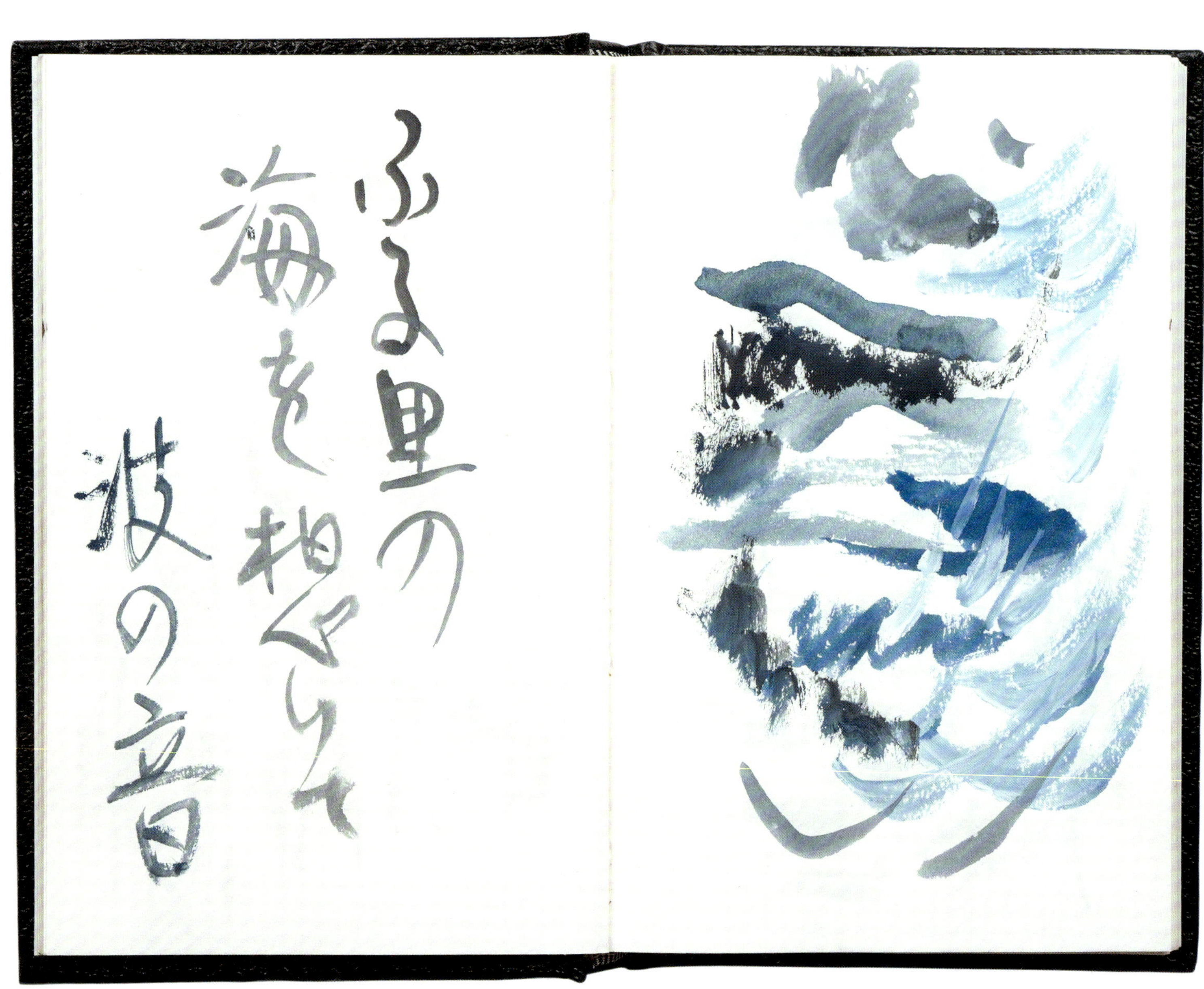

Of my hometown
I remember the ocean
The sound of the waves

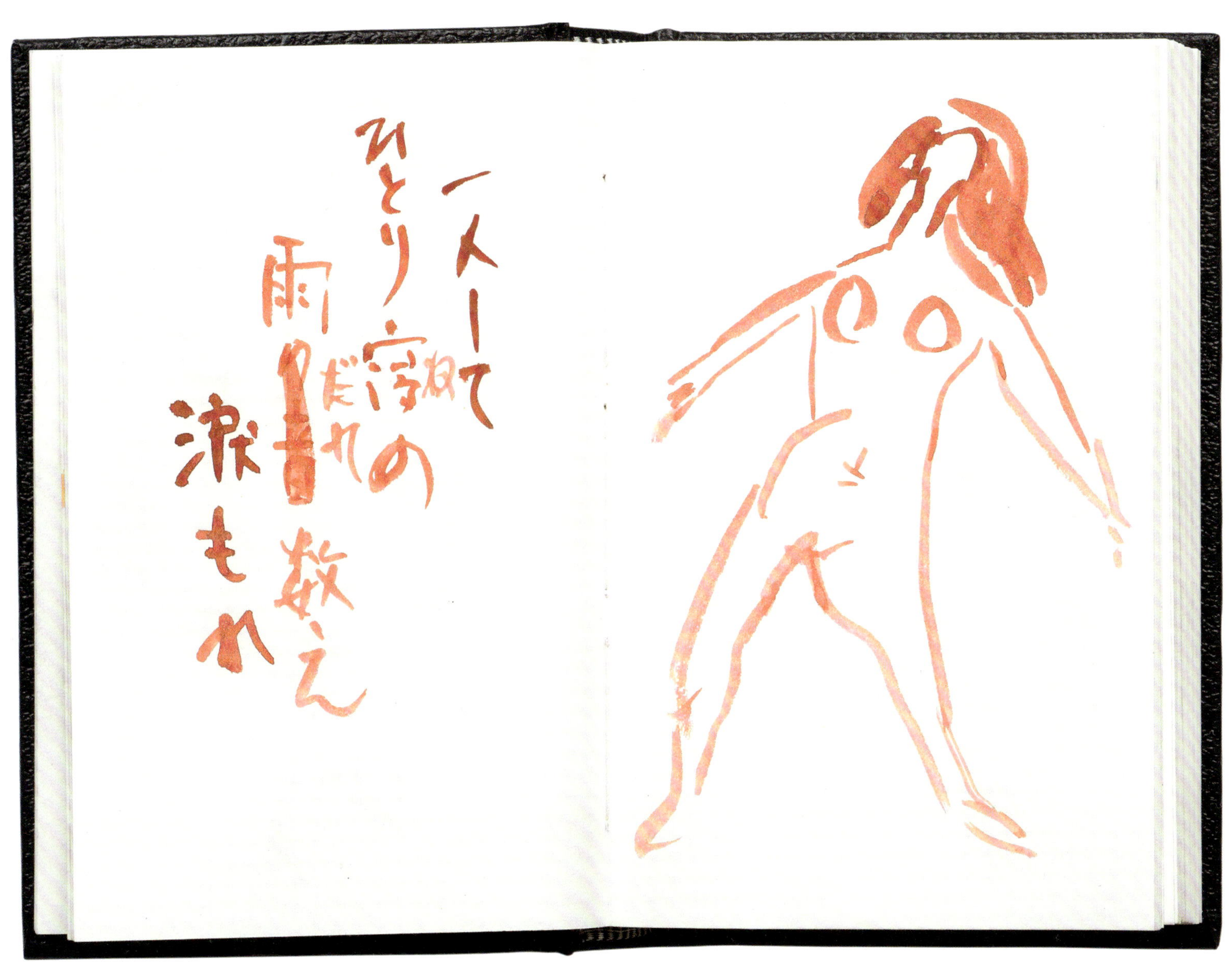

While lying alone
I count the falling raindrops
Tears flow from my eyes

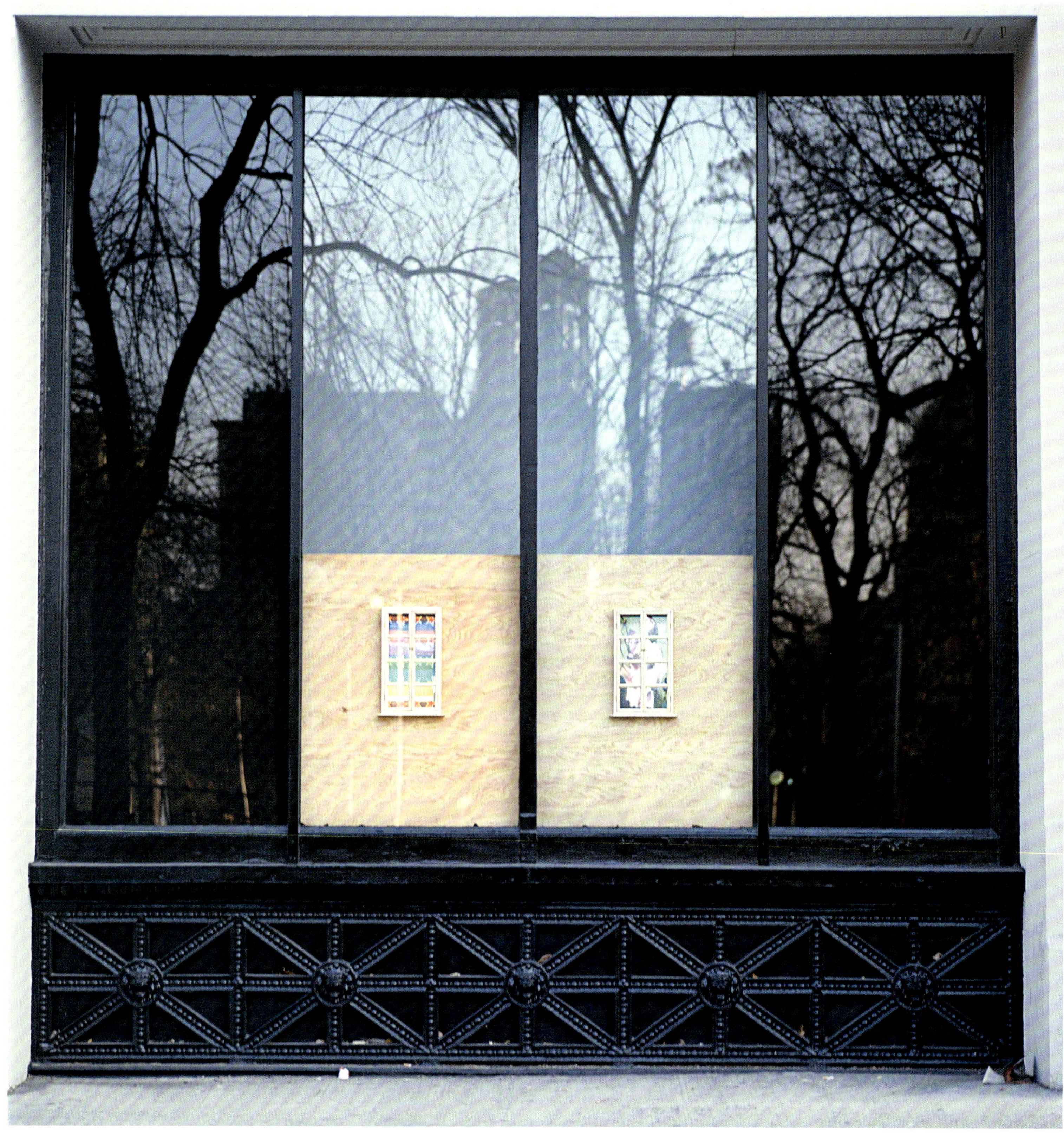

Peter Moore. Photograph of *Windows: Shigeko Kubota, "Meta-Marcel,"* Grey Art Gallery and Study Center, New York University, November 8–December 10, 1983. Left to right: *Meta-Marcel: Window (Stars)* and *Meta-Marcel: Window (Flowers)* (both 1983)

Hyundai Card

The exhibition is presented as part of The Hyundai Card Performance Series.

Major support is provided by the Jill and Peter Kraus Endowed Fund for Contemporary Exhibitions.

Generous funding is provided by the Lonti Ebers Endowment for Performance and the Sarah Arison Endowment Fund for Performance.

Photograph Credits

In reproducing the images contained in this publication, the Museum obtained the permission of the rights holders whenever possible. If the Museum could not locate the rights holders, notwithstanding good-faith efforts, it requests that any contact information concerning such rights holders be forwarded so that they may be contacted for future editions.

All works by Shigeko Kubota © 2021 Estate of Shigeko Kubota/Licensed by VAGA at Artists Rights Society (ARS), New York. Unless otherwise noted, all images of works by Shigeko Kubota are courtesy the Shigeko Kubota Video Art Foundation.

Courtesy Anthology Film Archives, New York: 24 (fig. 5); photo Robert Haller: 78, 81

© Artists Rights Society (ARS), New York/ADAGP, Paris/ Succession Marcel Duchamp: 47

Photo Peer Bode: 15

Courtesy Electronic Arts Intermix (EAI), New York: 14 (fig. 6), 28, 29, 94, 95

Courtesy Experimental Television Center, photo Evangelos Dousmanis: 13

Courtesy Galerie Hubert Winter, photo Simon Veres: 82

Photo Kris Graves: 11, 33, 64, 65, 67, 79, 96–99

Photo © 2021 Peter Harris Studio: 10, 26

Courtesy The Kitchen Archive, c. 1971–1999, The Getty Research Institute, Los Angeles: 41; photo Kris Graves: 34

Photo Eric Kroll: 52

Photo Achim Kukulies, Dusseldorf: 58, 66, 70

Photo Hollis Melton: 24 (fig. 6)

Photo Peter Moore. © 2021 Barbara Moore/Licensed by VAGA at Artists Rights Society (ARS), New York. Courtesy Paula Cooper Gallery, New York: 2, 30, 54, 100

Photo Peter Moore. Courtesy Barbara Moore and Paula Cooper Gallery, New York: 17, 18, 25, 38, 50, 56–57, 59, 71, 76–77, 84, 87, 92

Image © 2021 The Museum of Modern Art, Department of Imaging and Visual Resources: 12 (fig. 4); photo Peter Butler: 12 (fig. 3); photo John Wronn: 46

Courtesy the Niigata Prefectural Museum of Modern Art, photo Yukihiro Yoshihara: 27

Courtesy Takako Okamoto, Estate of Takehisa Kosugi, photo Hiroshi Naruse: 39

Photo Stephan Reusse: 53

Photo © 2021 Bobby Rogers for Walker Art Center, Minneapolis: 40

© 2021 Sonic Arts Union. Courtesy Mary Lucier: 23

Photo © 2021 Stedelijk Museum Amsterdam: 80, 93

Published in conjunction with the exhibition *Shigeko Kubota: Liquid Reality*, at The Museum of Modern Art, New York, August 21, 2021–January 1, 2022. Organized by Erica Papernik-Shimizu, Associate Curator, with the support of Veronika Molnar, Intern, Department of Media and Performance

The exhibition is presented as part of The Hyundai Card Performance Series.

Major support is provided by the Jill and Peter Kraus Endowed Fund for Contemporary Exhibitions.

Generous funding is provided by the Lonti Ebers Endowment for Performance and the Sarah Arison Endowment Fund for Performance.

Produced by the Department of Publications,
The Museum of Modern Art, New York
Hannah Kim, Business and Marketing Director
Don McMahon, Editorial Director
Marc Sapir, Production Director
Curtis R. Scott, Associate Publisher

Edited by Maria Marchenkova
Designed by Amanda Washburn
Production by Marc Sapir
Proofread by Rebecca Roberts
Printed and bound by Ofset Yapimevi, Istanbul

This book is typeset in TT Norms. The paper is 150 gsm GardaMatt Ultra and 120 gsm Munken Lynx Rough.

Published by The Museum of Modern Art
11 West 53 Street
New York, NY 10019-5497
www.moma.org

Library of Congress Control Number: 2021936675
ISBN: 978-1-63345-128-5

Distributed in the United States and Canada by
ARTBOOK | D.A.P.
75 Broad Street, Suite 630
New York, NY 10004
www.artbook.com

Distributed outside the United States and Canada by
Thames & Hudson
181A High Holborn
London WC1V 7QX
www.thamesandhudson.com

Printed and bound in Turkey

Front and back cover, front and back endpapers: Stills from *Niagara Falls I*. 1985. Four-channel standard-definition video (color, sound; approx. 31 min. each), ten cathode-ray tube monitors, plastic mirrors, plywood, water, and sprinkler system, 8 ft. × 54 in. × 8 ft. (243.8 × 137.2 × 243.8 cm). Shigeko Kubota Video Art Foundation

Back cover: Kubota in Piazza San Marco, Venice, 1972

p. 1: Untitled. 1988. Watercolor on paper, 6 × 4 in. (15.2 × 10.2 cm). Shigeko Kubota Video Art Foundation

p. 2: Peter Moore. Photograph of Kubota reflected in *Three Mountains* (1976–79), in her loft on Mercer Street, New York, 1979

pp. 106–11: Draft for the essay "Women's Video in the US and Japan," c. 1973. Published in *The New Television: A Public/Private Art*, ed. Douglas Davis and Allison Simmons (Cambridge, MA: MIT Press, 1977). Typescript in the collection of the Shigeko Kubota Video Art Foundation

p. 113: *Willow Tree and Wind*. n.d. Oil pastel on paper, 18 × 24 in. (45.7 × 61 cm). Shigeko Kubota Video Art Foundation

Trustees of The Museum of Modern Art

woman video in U.S. and Japan.

shigeko kubota

463 West street

apt A-512

1)

Man thinks, "I think, therefore I am".

I, a woman, feel, "I bleed, therefore I am."

Recently I bleed in half inch... 3 M or Sony..ten thousand feet long every month.

Man shoots me everynight... I can't resist.

I shoot him back at broad daylight with vidicon or tivicon flaming in over exposure.

Video is Vengeance and Victory of Vagina.

I like video, because it is heavy. Portapak and I travelled all over Europe and Japan without male accompanyment. Portapak tears down my shoulder, backbone and waist. I feel like a Soviet woman working at railway.

The first woman's video festival was held in 1972 September at Kitchen , Mercer Art Center, one of cradles of video art, which went down with the crumbling Broadway Central Hotel, one morning in the summer of '73. However I am one of many early video-birds, who would fondly reminisce the vibrant ecstasy of this premise, its openness, multi-sensory experience with Bars, Boutiques, and people, naive but good-humoured , non-elitistic atmosphere so rare in New York's career oriented art world.

Women's video festival opened with the award-winning shorts by Steina Vasulka. Close ups of her face, or a part of face, twitching and grimacing according to the "Let It Be" song. Somewhere behind its humour and satire I feel certain "tristesse", which Steina might not like to reveal, but which penetrates into my socks like spring snow.

"Lesbian Mother", by David Sasser and Queer Blue Light Video, is openly provocative. Three or four mothers living communally and raising children in a small apartment in urban environment, are trying to teach their kids that they should keep pride and dignity, although (?) mothers are un-wed, lesbian and on welfare. Jackie Cassen, pioneer in Light Art in the sixties, who shot street scenes and caught bar-full of men watching baseballl , while three Americans landed on moon and erased that valuable video documentary, showed tender portrait of tigerly lady at N.Y. Avantgarde : Charlotte Moorman. While Charlotte was performing Yoko Ono's cut piece (audience come on the stage and rip off performer's dress), Jackie Cassen made a beautiful tape delay of few seconds, which amplified and accentuated the latent feminism of Yoko's work, which was composed in 1963 before our movement.
The Rape Tape (by "under one roof") showed three courageous young women on camera, who spoke out to describe the horrible experience of being raped in first person and morever dialectically analized male mentality which award the crime with voyeristic reportage. Suzan Milano, who organized this successful festival with tireless Shridar Bapat , showed an old circus woman, who spent her whole life to satisfy male voyerism by exposing her tattoos, which covered her body ,wall to wall. A miserable example of conditioned womanhood, craving for the triple self exploitation. Festival concluded with Live video and dance by Elsa Tambellini and Judith Scott. Judith danced , while TV camera was attached on her body. Camera picks up various image at Kitchen, such as; other dancers, audience, floor and ceiling or monitors and these images were shown live at monitors, mixed with Elsa's powerful images of working men: eg . construction worker drilling holes , or meat butcher working with meat-grinding machienes. 12 monitors were lined up like a

military parade.

THe second annual Video Festival (1973) was enlarged into 57 artists and covered by a woman reporter from CBS evening news. Significantly many women invaded the last bastion of male technocrats, the intense interplay with electronic video synthesis. Olivia Tappan, Meyer, Kubota, Vasulka, Klein, Jane Wright, Louise Etra, Doris Chase etc did use various modes of electronic image generation, often combined with music and dance.

Shirley Clarke, who made many successful feature length films, such as Connections, Cool World, or Jason, suddenly gave up film completely and plunged into video. She is reputed to have said that video was her new penis... and she learned subtraction well. She scooped from the wide range of video technology, only those parts which cannot be done on film, in sharp contrast to many other video artists, who use video as a Ersatz-film. She converted whole penthouse of Hotel Chelsea into cybernated toy box. Three rooms, one terrace, three stages of roof top gardens are interconnected in video and audio in a counter-watergate manner and weird people of Chelsea hotel got wired to do strange things each other. Magnificient view of New York and Hudson River as a background scenery, people experiment here new psycho-therapy, a new kind of High Life instead of High Art, and not only artists, but also architect, environmentalist, psychologist, sociologist, socialist, and doctor will see the glimpse of future life and art in the post-industrial era. Wendy Clarke and several devoted young people are also strong creative input to this essentially needed luxury.

Behind the success of Video Movement (male and female), there are hidden devotion of women organisers, who worked hard without material reward such as Phyllis Gershuny and Beryl Korot of the Radical Software or Dorothy Chiesa and Olivia Tappan of WGBH, Boston. So is the case in Japan.

Fujiko Nakaya is the official representative of Video-Hiroba, the only video group, male and female, in Japan. Her father was an embodyment of "art and technology" by being a prominent research scientist on snow and also a widely read essaist. Miss Nakaya went school in Washington D.C. and was thoroughly introduced to the circle of Rauschenberg, David Tudor and Billy Kluever. She was instrumental in realizing multi-million dollar Pepsi-EAT Pavillion at Expo 70 in Osaka, Japan. In her conceptually inclined video tape , she tries and tries hard to let an egg stand up on a flat table. Lyrical flow of time is made visible by the accompaning music of Taji-Mahal Traveller's s[illegible]

Miss Idemitsu, who lives in Los Angeles as Mrs. Sam Francis, and lives in Tokyo at the same time as a heiress of oil concern made a videotape , titled simply "a work of a woman". It shows the close up of a male genital for 15 minutes. However, the concentration into this picture makes you think that you are watching a medieval SUMIE painting, which draws high mountain, deep water, a hermit looking up a full moon. The reason can be purely technical. Low definition, and grainy picture of porta-pak made this picture of male genital looks like a century old rice paper eaten up by worms.

Miss Michishita's Videotape has a long English title, "Being a woman in Japan, liberation within a Family". Miss Michishita studied journalism at University of Wisconsin a few years ago and experienced art and life in New York downtown. She is currently the organiser of cultural events at American Embassy in Japan, which has shown quite a few American video art pieces in the recent years.
Miss Michishita's tape, maybe reflecting her journalistic background, is of documentary nature. She goes to her home town, a small town in central Japan. Family is in crisis. Male member got sick and hospitalized. All female members got together and discuss what to do. At one point her mother said:

"Woman can do everything, what man does...
we just do it better..."

That is the difference.

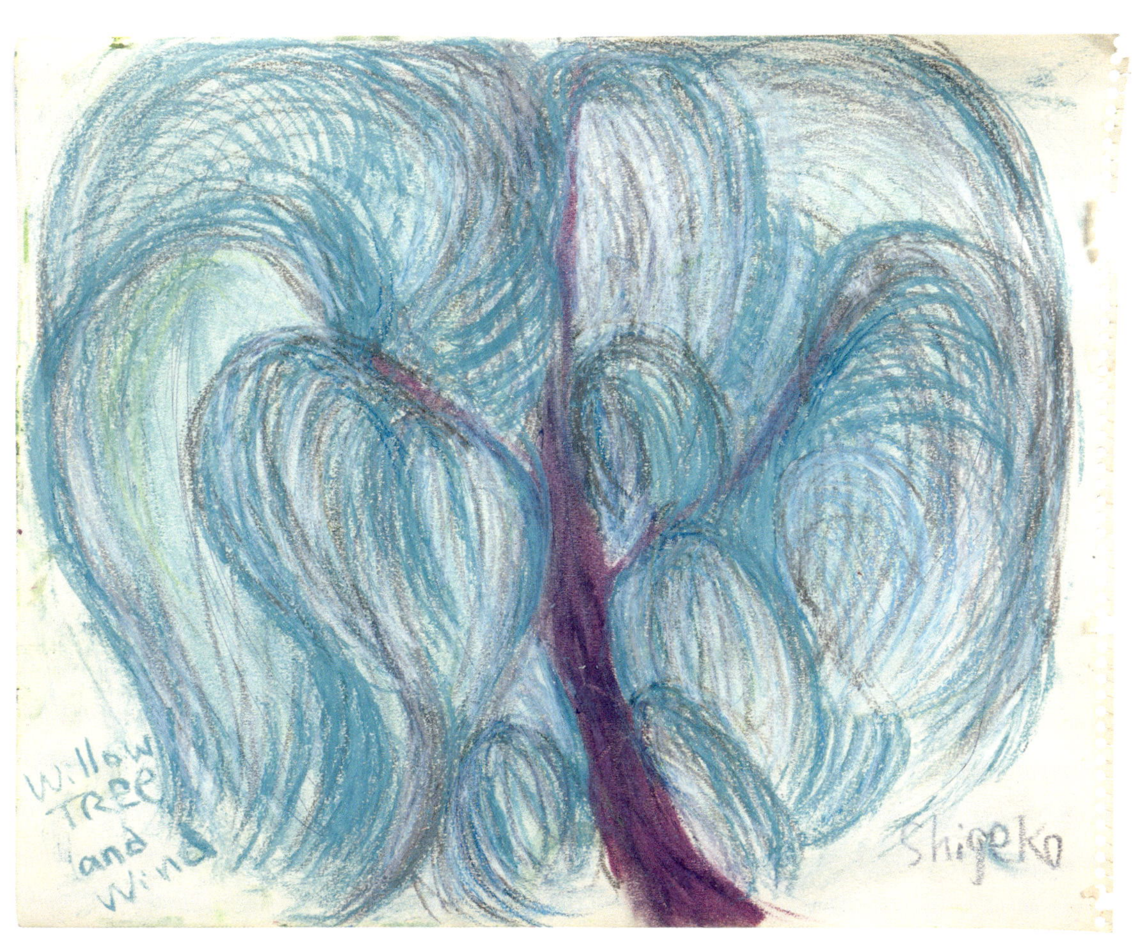
Willow TREE and Wind
Shigeko

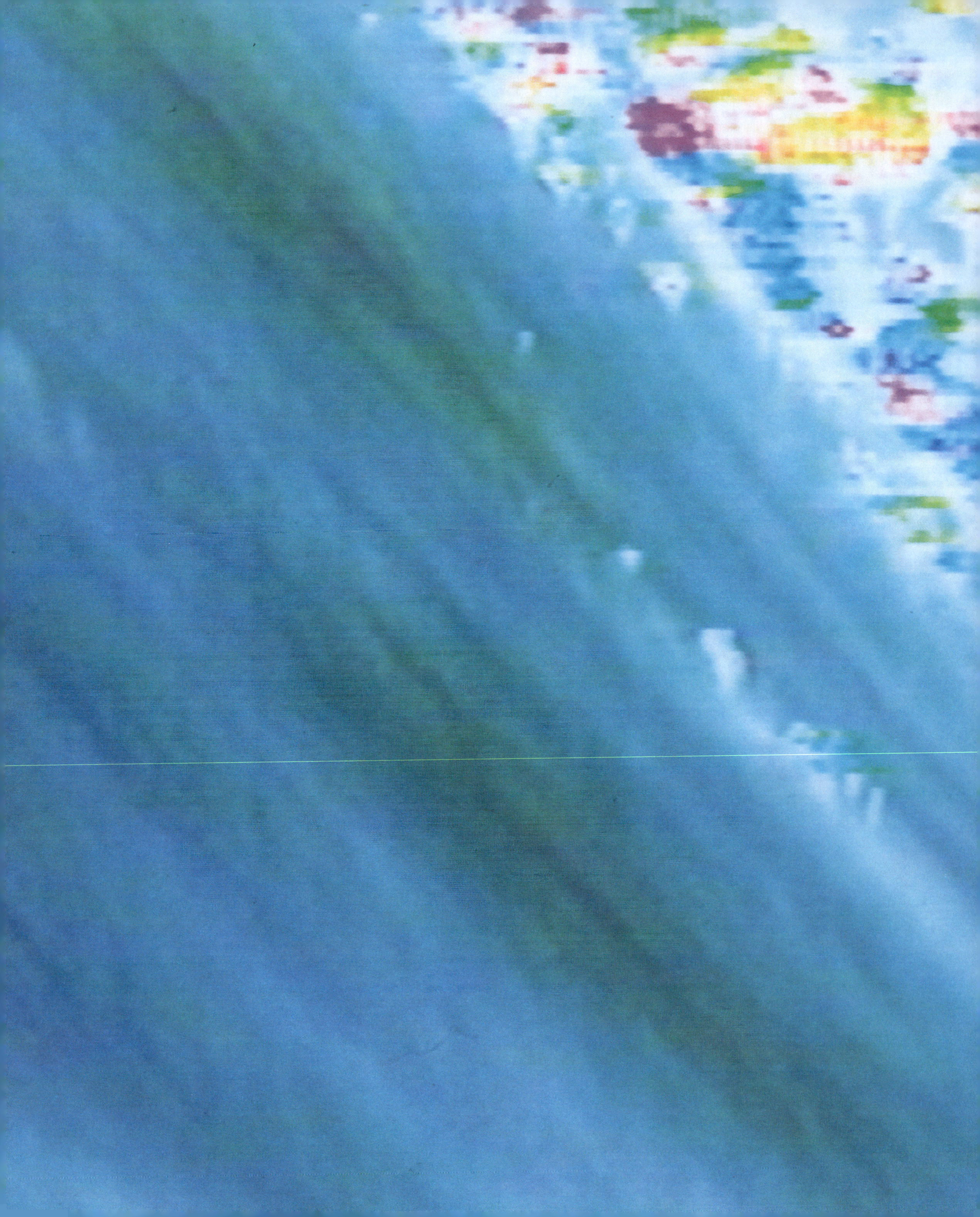